PERSONAL ASSIGNMENT

Joyce Norman

Personal Assignment

A Newspaperwoman's Search
for
The Good News

FLEMING H. REVELL COMPANY

Old Tappan, New Jersey

Library of Congress Cataloging in Publication Data

Norman, Joyce.
  Personal assignment.

    1. Norman, Joyce. 2. Conversion. I. Title.
BV4935.N59A3   248'.24 [B]   73–16193
ISBN 0–8007–0639–0

TO
My Mother
who never lost faith in me

Contents

Foreword

It is always an occasion to celebrate when anyone meets Jesus Christ. When, as with Joyce Norman, *growth* goes on, the celebration never needs to end.

I have known her from the day she celebrated her first year of Christian life. We are comfortable friends now, because her honesty with God and her continuing growth leave her free to be a friend.

Knowing her has helped me more than she will ever guess. For one thing, our first meeting enabled me to recognize a little of how I must have "mowed people down" when I was a new believer. I met her at the end of a long, tiring speaking tour and her high spirits made me feel old and still more exhausted. Typical of any new child of God who has just experienced the exhilarating difference between light and darkness, she came on strong. On that first meeting Joyce was on an assignment to interview me. She had so much to say, I felt I should have been interviewing her.

Portions of *Personal Assignment* were written during those

first glorious exuberant years. Her exuberance is still valid, but it is, without distorting her normally attractive, enthusiastic personality, going inward—where Christ intends it to go. Inward exuberance deepens, fills up empty places, allowing love to go outward. Her walk with Him is still childlike and stimulating, but there is the welcome plus of deepening faith.

To be with her now is at once fun and restful. Joyce trusts Jesus Christ. If that sounds superficial, read it again: *Joyce Norman trusts Jesus Christ.* Therefore, I and her other friends are free to trust her with Him. When she latches onto an unusual idea, as we all do—instead of trying to set her straight, I talk it over with the God who has a straight line to her—which, of course, indicates that I may be growing a little, too.

It's no simple thing to work in the midst of the hectic, hard-hitting world of a large city newspaper and walk sensitively with Jesus Christ. She does it now with far greater ease than at first, because He is teaching her, as He longs to teach us all, that Christians are just people who have found out that they are *loved.*

I'm delighted that she has done this first book. Later on, she would not have been able to recapture the freshness, the open-road liberty you will find here. I am convinced it will not be her last. In all ways, Joyce Norman is just beginning—as is anyone who has caught on to the freeing fact that the Christian life is always a new beginning.

In these pages, your own concept of God will be enlarged if you know Him already. If you don't know Him, I believe you will want to when you have finished reading *Personal Assignment.*

— EUGENIA PRICE

Preface

This book could well be termed a diary or a notebook. It has no general theme other than "God is love." I felt the need to put down on paper thoughts, observations, and experiences I have had since my own discovery of God.

Some are very personal. Others humorous. But all true and every one from Him.

Life as a newspaper reporter is interesting, rewarding, tiring—and I love it. The fact that my stories wind up under the kitty's litter or line garbage pails has ceased to worry me.

When I first began my work, I was shocked that my feature stories were not cut out and tacked on people's walls, or in scrapbooks. A visit to a neighbor's home showed me the transiency of newspaper writing. Her cute little puppy had other uses for my full-color Sunday story!

But then I decided I would take another approach and attitude toward my work. In interviews, at my desk typing out a story, on the telephone, driving to an assignment, taking photographs—in it all I would look for God. I have not been disappointed.

—JOYCE NORMAN

Acknowledgments

So many people have been a part of the writing of this book. They are too numerous to name. But just for being there when I needed them I offer my thanks.

To my family who loved the old Joyce and continues to pour out love to me, I say more than thank you. They understand.

But in particular, I must thank my ex-roommate, Deni Featheringill, who prayed with me and for me as I wrote; Mel, who loved and strengthened me and kept urging me to "finish that book"; to Mrs. Irma Cruse, for her invaluable encouragement and understanding of what I was attempting to do; Janice Walker, who helped me with the tedious job of rewriting and editing and for "getting into the book" with me; and last, but by no means least, my friends Joyce Blackburn, for her encouraging "cheerleader" letters, prayers, and love; and Eugenia Price, whose wisdom and honesty challenged me to be a better writer. I owe her many lessons of love.

1

Up, Up, and Away

The alarm didn't get its full workout on this particular morning. I was wide-eyed at the first sound of it and lay in bed for a few minutes thinking of what lay ahead.

Weeks before, my editor had posed an assignment to me in the form of a question: "Want to go up in a balloon?"

My editor asked with such a deadpan expression I thought perhaps I was about to receive the "pink slip." But she came to my desk and explained that a balloonist was creating some conversation with his colorful balloon around Alabama—so why didn't I go up for a ride and write about the experience?

I contacted Sam, the balloonist, and he was happy to have me come for a ride in the clouds with him. Arrangements were set, our color photographer was told of the assignment and I began to do my homework—reading all I could on hot-air balloons. Looking back now, I believe I would have been wiser to have done my research *after* the flight.

Explanations of how propane gas is shot into the silk balloon to give it its lift and how a balloonist has no horizontal control at all — only vertical — brought many questions to mind. Sam could get us up and down, but where we floated would be left to the winds.

The day arrived and I drove to the take-off site, some flat farmland about thirty miles southeast of Birmingham. Friends and well-wishers had been telling me for days that I shouldn't do the balloon story. All agreed it was too risky for "just a newspaper article." But when I was a child Mother always overprotected me and overcautioned me about everything, so when I became an adult I wanted to do any adventurous thing that came up. Ballooning certainly turned out to be *one kind of an adventure!*

When I arrived, Sam and some friends were taking the balloon out of a box. My first thought was, "But it's so small." Once the aluminum and wooden gondola was set upright, the silk balloon was attached to it and Sam began the job of filling the balloon with heat from the gas tanks. Red orange flames shot into the red and yellow sphere and soon it righted itself. Sam yelled for me to hop in as the wind was beginning to move the balloon and was calling us to join it.

I approached the small gondola and said, "I can't do it." I began to agree with my friends that this *was* too much to risk for a story.

But our color photographer said, "Get in, Joyce. We've come all this way and even hired an airplane for aerial shots. Get in."

I really had no choice. I hopped in and helpers on the ground began to let go the tether line. Soon Sam and I were leaving ground behind us and he was pulling up the rope.

"Well," he said proudly, "we're free. We belong to the wind now. How do you like it?"

At intervals Sam let go with a burst of flame from the tank overhead and higher and higher we went. Before long the people on the ground looked like ants and I at last had to admit, "Sam, this is beautiful."

As we were traveling with the wind there was no sound. We floated over trees, housetops, freeways—all in an eerie silence. We had been up about ten minutes when Sam said, "Joyce, hold on. We have to go down in a hurry. One of the propane tanks aboard has a leak in it and if the gas gets to the flames, we've had it. I'm going to put us down in that corn-field over there."

I love corn, but envisioning myself landing in a field of it didn't do much for me. I did as I was told—held on. Sam pulled the rope that opened a twelve-foot slit in the balloon and we came down very rapidly. We hit the ground hard, the balloon dragged us about ten yards, turned on its side, and dumped us out. I love Alabama and was glad to be back on land again. Even that mouthful of southern soil tasted good.

Other than minor scratches on my knees and elbows, no damage was done to my body. Sam was okay, too, and we began rolling up the silk while waiting for the follow car to locate us.

Find us they did and we loaded up the balloon and headed back to meet the photographer, who had been left in a quandary because all he saw was the balloon drop suddenly out of sight behind some trees.

It wasn't until I returned to the office and sat down that what had happened hit me. Everybody had laughed about it after-ward, but then I got the full realization of what is known in anybody's jargon as "a close call."

I had ridden in a glider for a story, a helicopter, gone caving, spent three days alone on an island in the Caribbean, and other rather daring things, but that morning I had come closer to being wiped out than at any other time.

If the lethal, invisible gas had reached the flames, Sam and I would not have lived to tell the story — or me to write one. The moment of happening brought real fear, I'll admit. But I am amazed now at the calmness that came over me as we swiftly descended. I'm no Mary Marvel, but I didn't panic either. All Sam uttered as we dropped from the sky was a running patter of one sentence, "You okay, Joyce? You okay?"

"Right," I answered. "No worry." I only remember thinking one thing and that was, "I am with you alway" (Matthew 28:20). And that meant in a balloon, too.

I know full well before I invited God to take control of my life I would have gone to pieces in a situation like that. I'm not sure I wouldn't have tried to jump out. (Sam told me later he was afraid I might.)

So I sat at my desk, amazed at the control I had managed to have within me. I knew it all came from Him and I thanked Him. Had I panicked in that balloon the ending might not have been happy.

But it was, because I had come to a better appreciation of 2 Timothy 1:7, "For God hath not given us the spirit of fear; but . . . of a sound mind."

It never ceases to amaze me that God is in everything I do. As you share other experiences with me, perhaps you, too, will be able to see that He *is* with us always.

But let's start at the beginning.

2

Of Jump Ropes and Things

I was born to unsuspecting parents. Two teen-age sons made up the household when, at age forty-one, my mother was informed she could expect a blessed event. My forty-nine-year-old father considered the news anything but blessed.

But, sure enough, at 5 A.M. on a May 1, I entered this world to be named Joyce Ann. A nine-pound baby girl, my father soon made up his mind to keep me and let the blessed aspect develop.

Many people attribute what they are in part to their upbringing. I've known many people who use their young years as excuses for their adult behavior.

If a woman, and I know one, has a violent temper, she merely says, "Well, my mother had an awful temper and people say I'm just like her." Cop out!

"I'm insecure," says another. "We didn't have much when I was growing up and I feel my immaturity and insecurity stem from this." Hogwash!

I have no degree in psychology—just a B.S. in Speech and

English — so I speak from a lower rung of the layman's ladder.

In some cases, it is true, childhood experiences have been so traumatic and scary that there is a definite relationship to adult behavior.

But for the most part, at least, I believe we *are* what we *are* and what we make of our lives is up to us — and God. A great team effort. A beautiful togetherness! He says that through Him, "all things are possible" (Matthew 19:26), and since I invited Him into my life, I know this to be true. I cannot, nor do not, blame my childhood or my parents. I take full credit for every stupid, asinine thing I've ever done or will do in the future.

My own childhood was not one I would term completely happy. My father, however proud he was of me, soon discovered that a small child was wearing on a man of fifty-five. He began to drink heavily and I recall many, many evenings of loud talking in the kitchen with my mother always saying softly, "Don't talk so loud, Will. Joyce will hear you."

My father was not a violent man. When he drank, however, he was very argumentative and these one-sided arguments between him and my mother made me sick to my stomach. Many times I'd sit on the back steps with my hands over my ears to muffle the noise inside. How I hated those sounds and I wondered if all families were like mine. Sometimes I got so nervous I couldn't eat.

At other times my father was the funniest, most charming man in the world. He loved the circus and so did I. This we had in common and I looked forward to going with my father to the railroad yards to watch them unload the animals.

Then we'd head for the circus and my father would laugh and hold me up high so I could see the clowns. This was his favorite part, I think — mine, too, because he laughed a lot.

I grew up in an older neighborhood; consequently, there

were few children with whom I could play. So I made my own world of make-believe and into this world I escaped every day after school.

I had one neighborhood friend my age, Ralph, but he always wanted to play war games. The day he insisted I go first off our garage in a "parachute" he'd made out of an old torn sheet caused my mother to say, "Watch out for Ralph."

No sympathy emitted from her for my bruises and scratches, however, and the old trusty peach-tree limb got a good work-out on the back of my already tender legs.

The friendship between Ralph and me came to an abrupt halt the afternoon Mother saw us in the highest limbs of our chinaberry tree attired in nothing but our underwear. The fact that I was Jane and he was Tarzan had no effect on her except to bring forth a lecture about eight-year-olds not cavorting about outdoors in their undies.

But Mother didn't understand Ralph was my *only* friend. I really didn't like him much anyway, so I found a new playmate — Mrs. Gibbons — dear, sweet seventy-five-year-old Mrs. Gibbons, who lived in the big house next door. Mother always thought I was bothering her. Our many afternoons together are special memories to me.

She and her husband once lived in Egypt and every day she would bring out faded photos and trophies of their travels. She talked, but most important to me, I talked and she actually listened. For her it wasn't easy because at this point in my life I became a stutterer. It's funny I didn't stutter much when I was with her.

That white-haired sweet lady never knew, I'm sure, what treasures she brought into my life as a child who needed attention. It was a great thrill to know happiness could be found behind the gate separating our houses.

Mother always took me to the movies on Saturday, gave me

money for popcorn and candy, and left me there for the day to watch Captain Marvel, the Green Hornet, and Superman serials. One Saturday I ate a whole forty-nine-cent bag of candy by myself and was sick through the last episode of Captain Marvel. (I still don't know how it ended, but am quite sure the captain came out the hero.)

My imagination was wild and I was every character in all the movies I'd seen. I was a tough Dale Evans, I'll tell you that. My father's sawhorse, his oversized Stetson hat, and me singing, "Happy Trails" would have made Trigger envious. I put many miles on that old splintered sawhorse, but the trails weren't always happy.

Looking back, I see myself as a very lonely child. I never said it, but I spent half my time doing things that were obvious "Look-at-me's." I craved attention and really didn't mind the peach-tree-limb ordeals because for that moment I was my mother's center of attention.

Don't misunderstand me. I never (I wasn't *that* stupid) did things in order for a spanking to evolve. No way! Mother wielded a mean tree limb and although I have no physical scars, I can still recall that sting on the back of my legs.

My father let me have a piece of chalk from his carpenter's box and I marked off a giant hopscotch game on the front sidewalk. After tiring of this sport, I'd pick up the jump rope and see how many times I could jump without getting tangled in the rope. I got to be pretty good with that red-handled rope and used to watch cars go by on busy College Avenue and think to myself, "I bet there's a Hollywood talent scout in one of those cars and he'll see me jumping rope without missing and he'll take me to California and make a star out of me. Yep, this jump rope will get me to Hollywood."

Most kids had a favorite toy. Not me. I had Ralph. I got my first doll when I was thirteen years old. Don't ask me why.

That's just the moment in my life when I wanted one. So a skinny thirteen-year-old wagged around a doll. Who laughed? Not me.

My wanting a doll just sort of happened. I was downtown one day around the first of December and wandered into the toy department. Dolls of every variety lined shelves and I only gave them a passing glance.

But then I looked down and there in a tiny bassinet was a doll that looked just like a real baby. She was dressed in white, had short legs and dimpled knees, and had little white shoes and socks on. Her eyes were closed and she looked so soft and cuddly lying there. I picked up the price tag and let it drop quickly—fifty dollars.

That doll for me? No way. Christmases at our house were a game and something to wear. We didn't have fifty dollars in our budget for an emergency, so although the sign read, PLEASE DO NOT TOUCH, I picked up that tiny sleeping baby doll and hugged her.

I told Mother about the doll and she told me what I already knew—that I couldn't have it. But she was warm and loving in telling me and even though I wanted that doll so, I understood.

We always had Christmas on the evening of the twenty-fourth even though I protested loudly to wait until Christmas morning to open presents.

This Christmas of my thirteenth year, Mother informed me we could wait until morning. Even though our tree wasn't surrounded with wrapped presents, I was excited when I went to bed on Christmas Eve.

My youngest brother, Gardner, and his wife, Jo, came over about 8 A.M. and we opened presents. I got the usual necessary clothes items and thought Christmas was pretty slim. Then Mother asked me to look in the closet. There in that small cubicle was *the doll,* bassinet and all.

I can never remember being happier but I turned and asked Mother, "How?" She said she had been able to buy just the doll and Jo had made the bassinet and clothes. Mine even had a satin coverlet! I still have that doll and it reminds me of how much my mother really loved me.

I guess it's no big deal, but I always wanted a stocking hung at Christmas. Mother never put one up. I know it wasn't because she didn't care. She had raised two boys and this had never been a ritual with them so she just didn't think about it.

I got my first Christmas stocking at age twenty-five and filled it myself with all the things I thought were supposed to go in stockings. Now, in loving memory of Christmases that can never be relived, I hang a stocking every year.

In everything, I still believed there was something "out there" beyond what I knew and I longed to discover it.

My brothers were both married and gone from home, so in a sense I was an only child. Gardner lived in Fort Worth and Dub was a captain in the air force. His visits were like MacArthur landing in the Philippines. He was so handsome in his uniform and from my height he was a giant and a real war hero. He spent the war stationed on Galápagos Island near Ecuador and saw nothing more fierce than one of the many large turtles that inhabit the island.

But his occasional visits were special events and I would talk loudly and exaggeratedly at school about my war-hero brother home from the battle. Once he brought me a whole box of Fleer's bubble gum and I sold each piece for twenty-five cents. With the money I made from my bubble-gum racket I bought a little tool kit with hammer, pliers, nails, and a carpenter's apron at the dime store.

I guess I was trying to do something to really make my father happy and proud of me. He gave me some old pieces of lumber and I nailed them together and showed them to him every night when he came home.

Depending on his mood he was either excited that I'd driven a straight nail or I'd get — "Show me tomorrow. I'm tired tonight." But it was fun when he held up two nailed-together boards and said, "Now, that's a real carpenter for you. Look at how sturdy this is."

Mother would look at me and wink. These times pleased her, too, and I know now she realized how special they were to me. Mother was liaison officer between my father and me. She would have long talks with me and always she would defend him.

Before the depression, my father had accrued quite a lot of land, was in the contracting and building business, and doing very well. The depression wiped him out and with it took away most of his enormous drive and creativity.

So he had to take a job with the railroad. Car inspector, I believe his title was. All he did was look under train cars to see if there was any damage. Not a very challenging job for a man with as much innate imagination and humor as my father possessed.

That man was really funny and he didn't have to try to be. His quick ad libs brought laughter to any group in which he found himself.

He was even funny sometimes when he was angry. Mother would send him to the grocery store and if he bought something that cost too much she would say something to him about it. His face would get red and he'd pick up the item, stand at the back door and say, "Alright, just throw it in the back alley."

If he had thrown everything he threatened to in our alley, the garbage truck would never have been able to get through. That got to be a standard family joke — the only one I can remember.

I recall once when Mother was living with me in Alabama she was taking some medicine that made her very ill. She was in the hospital and had tubes in both arms. I walked up to her bed and she lay so still I started to ring for a nurse. Then she opened her eyes, looked up at me and said, "Know what you can do with this medicine? Throw it in the back alley!"

But that job at the railroad was not only not challenging, it didn't pay well either. I was constantly reminded that we must live on $175 a month.

We lived in a three-room duplex and my "room" was the screened back porch. I do not recall fondly cold nights in Texas—even with the kitchen door open.

However, I took pride in my back-porch room because until then I had slept on the sofa in the living room. Dad nailed canvas over the screened-in part and Mother said I could fix it up any way I wanted.

So I painted the linoleum floor box-car red (Dad got the paint free at the railroad) and Mother dyed sheets navy blue for curtains and a spread.

Because of the free paint, red was sort of my basic color. I was in junior high now and remembered a friend's bedroom was covered in bright red carpeting. The pile on my linoleum wasn't as soft as her floor but the smell of that fresh paint was beautiful to me. I chose navy blue only because I couldn't think of anything else to go with red.

I plastered the one wall I had with magazine cutouts of movie stars. There wasn't a half inch of bare space on that wall.

Alan Ladd, Guy Madison, Shirley Temple, Roy Rogers— they were all there looking down at me. Oh, the games of let's pretend I played with them. Once Zachary Scott came to Fort Worth to visit his aunt. I called her number and he actually answered the phone. Nobody believed me but I talked about that for weeks.

A sawhorse with a board across it was my first desk and a nail keg was my chair. Red floor, pictures all over the wall. My room was my castle. It was better than super. It might not have been as sharp as my friends' rooms but it beat sleeping on the sofa in the living room. *My* room. I loved it!

3

A Walk Down an Aisle

My mother and father went to the church they had gone to before I was born. But all my friends from school went to one near our house, so I started going there.

At the age of fifteen I thought to myself one summer, "Before school starts again I've got to have my tonsils out and get saved."

That was the order of importance I put on these two chores. My Sunday-school teacher had been hinting for over a year that one person in our class was not going to go to heaven with the rest. She would look in my direction and say, "You know where *she's* going!"

That teacher was something else. She assumed because all the other kids' parents attended that church the whole class but me was saved. She really zeroed in on me.

She put a check mark in red ink by the Sunday-school lesson every Sunday. When I got mine back, I'd find tracts stuffed between the pages about "Lost Souls," "Where Will You Spend Eternity?" or "It's Hot in Hell." I never read them and got mad because she was so sneaky about the whole business.

The minister stopped me in the hall once and asked me if I didn't think I ought to join the church.

"The young people need you. You could add much to our church," he said, "and the choir always needs new voices."

I look back now and can appreciate his talking to me, but he never once asked me about a relationship with God. I've often wondered why.

However, it's that teacher standing behind a small rostrum that bugged me. One Sunday she said, "We all love each other in this class. Wouldn't it be a shame if we couldn't all spend eternity together?"

Then she would go into a lengthy description of her concept of the hot place and I really felt uncomfortable. But then the thought of having my tonsils out made me uncomfortable, too, so I decided I would get the big surgery out of the way first and then pacify my rip-roaring teacher and get saved.

The tonsillectomy went as well as could be expected considering the screaming teen-ager my doctor had to work with.

My first Sunday back at Sunday school was full of talk about sore throats and how "brave" I'd been through the whole ordeal. I had an idea liars went to that hot place, too.

The second Sunday we had an evangelist and he came on strong about sinners being robbers. "If you're not a child of God's, then you are stealing His air that you breathe, His food you eat, et cetera." Then he ended his sermon with a talk about hell for the unsaved and all one had to do was walk down the aisle and he would be home free.

I would have gone down anyway, but my teacher elbowed me and said, "Joyce, you better go. You might not have another chance." I really didn't even like her.

So, on the last verse of "Just As I Am," I hit the aisle and was met by the minister, who said, "We've been praying about you for a long time. Glad to have you join our church."

I filled out a card and was baptized that night. There was no emotion involved. No intellect. No nothing! I was a member of a church but just as lost as I had been at breakfast that morning. I had no idea what it meant to "confess your sins." I knew nothing of repentance. Asking God to come into my heart was foreign to me.

And as I lay in bed that night and thought back over the day's activities I felt nothing but relief that I wouldn't have to go to hell. I had no desire to talk to God. The thought of reading the Bible never entered my head.

No one, including the minister, had asked me to share what had happened in my life. No one explained "how to believe." I just walked an aisle and joined a church. I hate to confess to such naiveté, but I honestly felt this was all there was to the church thing. I was disappointed and disillusioned.

Now being a member of the fold, I was voted in as president of just about every youth group in the church. I was put in charge of Fellowship Time after Sunday evening services. We had real productions in that basement — talent shows, plays, games. The thought of a Bible study was something I probably would have laughed about. That church was my country club and I was an active participant.

The real thing that got me to that church in the first place and kept me coming afterward was my steady fellow. I never had any trouble getting out of the house for a date. "Charles and I are going to church." Mother thought it was great that I was so interested in church and never balked when I sailed out the door almost every night.

There was a meeting of some kind or another at the church all the time. If not that, then choir rehearsal, a party, or going to a nursing home and doing skits for the residents.

I think it's great to be in a church where so much is going on and kids are coming, but even then I felt something was missing. Had we had some honest-to-goodness Bible studies and prayer sessions, I just might have discovered what was missing.

I carried a Bible and even got a certificate for never missing Sunday school for a whole year. But I never read my Bible. I was far too busy being a church member.

4

Leaving Tracks Behind Me

I zoomed through high school and at times I envied my friends their big houses. I'd spend the night at their homes but I never worked up the nerve to bring anybody to my back-porch room. High school brings back no memories at all—good or bad. If not for a rolled-up diploma and my senior picture in the annual I would have my doubts that I was ever there at all.

Then it came time for college. At the beginning of the summer after high-school graduation, I mentioned it at dinner (we called it supper) one night and silence was my answer.

Then one day in July, my father asked me to ride to the store with him. This was unusual because he always liked to go alone. He could sneak a few drinks and hope Mother wouldn't find out.

We drove around the corner and stopped and for the first time I can remember, my father actually talked to me as an adult.

"Your mother and I know how much you want to go to college," he said, "but you know we can't afford it. I'll help you if you really think you can learn something. I'll do carpenter work on Saturdays and if you can get a part-time job I think we can make it. You'll have to live at home but at least you'll get to go to that college you're always talking about."

My sixty-six-year-old father wiped away every bad memory I ever had in those moments in that car. He loved me! He never spoke the words as far as I can recall, but he proved it.

So, come September, I was a member of the freshman class at Texas Wesleyan College in Fort Worth, Texas. No frosh beanie was ever worn as proudly as mine. I knew the cost.

Within a few short months my father died and I think it was at this point I realized I truly loved him. And one thing was obvious to me—regardless of his words or actions, *I* had never told him I loved him either.

I finished college with the aid of scholarships, workships, and dropping out a year to work and then return. Besides my own desire to get that diploma I knew now how much my father had wanted me to have it. I had overheard him say to Mother one night after my first week in college, "Well, at least one of our children will have a college education. Now if Joyce will keep up those grades, I'll work extra hard to put her through."

I kept my end of the bargain, too—out of school at noon and on to work in the afternoons. During my four years at TWC I worked at a dairy, typed (pitifully) for an accountant, worked in a photo studio, waited tables, and babysat.

I was just an average student but my grades improved greatly my senior year when I moved into the dorm and roomed with Marge, an *A* student. I had obtained a work scholarship that required me to live on campus and this was my favorite year.

That was also the year I got campused for two weeks.

One winter evening it began to really snow and by midnight the beautiful white covered everything. Marge and I looked out our windows and both thought the same thing: "Why stay in? Let's do something."

I was the only girl in Dan Hall who had a car. My father had left me his old 1952 Hudson and it was parked in front of the dorm. Outside our window was a nifty fire escape and Marge and I got the bright idea to crawl down our handy exit, get in my car, and drive across campus to Ann Hall, our rival.

We drove through the still night with the car lights out, pulled up behind Ann Hall and climbed their fire escape to the third floor. We opened a window and crawled in, headed for the laundry room where we overloaded four washing machines with soap powder, put quarters in, and returned unnoticed to my car.

Back and snug in our room we laughed about our big caper. At 2 A.M. a loud knock at our door awakened us. It was the dorm mother summoning us to her room. The dorm mother at Ann Hall had called.

It seems shoes and car tires leave evidence in the snow and it wasn't difficult to pinpoint the culprits. But why was everybody excited because soapsuds practically washed away the third floor of Ann Hall?

The Dean of Women campused Marge and me and although we hated being confined to our room, we loved what we'd pulled off on that other dorm.

I was due to go visit my mother that weekend and I telephoned her that I couldn't make it. "See, Mother, I've gotten this honor. I've been campused and that means I can't leave the grounds for two weeks."

Bless her, she thought it was really an award I'd won, until I told her years later. I didn't get the peach-tree limb but her look stung in much the same manner.

I graduated in August and when the president of TWC

handed me my diploma, I looked at Mother and never saw her look happier. Although she never said, I believe she was thinking the same thing as I — wouldn't my father be proud!

Diploma in hand, I confidently set forth — to teach? Me, a teacher? The thought even made *me* laugh. But thanks to a wise counselor at the beginning of my senior year I had taken the necessary education courses to obtain a teaching certificate. With a degree in drama I wouldn't have gotten far without that teaching certificate. I wasn't ready for Hollywood and vice versa. "So I'll teach for a year," I said.

My first job after graduation was teaching ninth-grade English and mine is a duplicate of most first-year teachers' stories. Greenhorn teacher, teen-agers, and English. This trio seems to have trouble mixing well. But they learned some things that year and I learned a great deal.

For part-time work I did a children's television program on Saturdays and full time during the summer months. I had two little puppets and a studio full of kids. We all got along fine and had a successful year.

Sammy Skunk and Prissy Pack Rat were on television two times a day and soon became household words among the younger set.

Sammy is a six-year-old tease who never ages. Prissy is a shy, soft-spoken four-year-old and will never see five. They both were born on my sister-in-law's sewing machine over ten years ago but will always be "my children."

Little boys easily identified with Sammy and mothers would write in that everything Sammy said, their sons would pick up. When Prissy would tell a story or do a commercial, Sammy would edge her out of the way and try to take over. To me they were real and although I did the voices for them, I was completely divorced from the two little characters.

I would go home following the early morning taping of our first show and watch the program with Mother. I would really laugh at Sammy and many of the things he did surprised me. I never thought, "Gee, Joyce, you're funny." Sammy was and still is another person to me and I could objectively sit and enjoy the program.

Mother felt the same way about them. One day after a program she got very quiet. She didn't have much to say to me. Finally, I asked her what was wrong. She looked me straight in the eyes and very seriously said, "Sammy never lets Prissy get a word in. Bless her heart, she starts to say something and he interrupts her." She wasn't angry at *me,* just a little down on Sammy.

But this six-year-old skunk with furry hair made out of a commode lid cover had his effect on children. One mother called me at the TV station to say her six-year-old son had to wear glasses and he was very upset about it. "Can Sammy do something to help?" she asked.

The next day Sammy Skunk did both shows sporting the biggest pair of glasses I could find. Prissy kept asking to wear them and Sammy would say, "Nope. They're mine and nobody else can put 'em on. Only important, intelligent people wear glasses. Besides, I can see better with 'em on."

The next week I received a note in the mail reading: "Dear Sammy: My son loves his glasses and we're having trouble getting them off him at bedtime. Thanks."

Before we began to tape our shows we did our hour-long programs live and any mistakes we made were miles away and could never be reclaimed.

To me, the most horrible thing that happened during the live programs happened to (who else?) Prissy.

I had a monitor behind the set so I could see what was happening. I wore headphones to get instructions from the director as to how much time we had left, when to do a commercial, or when to go into a cartoon.

The whole routine was rather like rubbing your tummy and patting your head at the same time. I didn't watch the monitor much as I was too busy working Sammy and Prissy and thinking what to say next. (We had no script. It was all ad lib.)

Sam and Priss were pantomiming a record when over the headphones came a rather tense voice saying, "Joyce, get Prissy down—quick!" I turned my head and looked in the monitor and there was Prissy, singing her little heart out with her left button eye hanging by a single thread.

On TV sets across Fort Worth and Dallas, Prissy made a hasty exit and Sammy covered by saying she had to check on some cookies she had in the oven. I guess no one noticed. I got no mail.

Sammy and Prissy now sit on the sofa in my study and as I write they watch me. When I get in a rough spot with an idea I look up and say, "Okay, you two. Where do I go from here?" They just look back at me as if to say, "Look, Mom, we're retired. Keep plugging, you'll get it."

How I do love those little guys with the button eyes!

Many of my friends began to move to other cities on different jobs and soon the wanderlust hit me. I had some friends in Alabama so I thought I would write and apply to teach there. It wasn't long before I learned I had been accepted to teach high-school English and speech in Birmingham.

It was difficult saying good-bye to Mother. I had never been away from home and I knew I would leave her lonely. But I promised to come back at every vacation time and write often, so the blow was softened.

With one box, two suitcases, and my puppets, I headed for Alabama.

5

Behold, I Stand at the Door

School was fine. I wasn't quite as green as that first year and my students were great. Many of them are close friends now and although it makes me feel older, I love it when they bring their own children by for a visit.

During that first year I became involved in a civic theater group and discovered I really loved acting. A couple of leads and I thought to myself, "Well, old schoolroom, I'll soon be leaving you for the silver screen."

After every rehearsal the cast and crew hung around the theater and somebody went out for sandwiches and beer. I didn't drink. Never had. I was adamantly against it because of its effect in my home.

But one evening I recall asking someone to bring me a beer. Quite a discovery. I liked it! Play followed play and acting got into my blood. Actually, my blood was made up of 90 percent theater and 10 percent alcohol.

In the middle of a rehearsal I received a call from Mother saying simply, "Went for a checkup today. I have cancer. Surgery is set for day after tomorrow."

I explained to the director and took off for Texas. The doctor's prognosis was bleak. "She has less than a year to live. We didn't get to it in time."

When she was able to travel I flew her to Birmingham to live with me. She seemed happy here and actually began to improve. Mother fooled everybody, especially the doctor, by living four years past his prediction. But she suffered. I could see it in her eyes, and as the months went by the only thing that seemed to help were the increased doses of morphine.

For me the need to drink increased, also. And I did nothing to suppress it. I had a "valid reason" and never let myself think otherwise.

Oh, I suppose, to be perfectly honest, there was more than one reason. I hated to see my mother suffer and alcohol deadened the pain it brought me. But really to be honest, I felt resentment that I had the full responsibility of Mother. The unmarried-daughter-is-the-natural-one-to-care-for-Mother syndrome set in good. I felt like a real martyr and every time I paid a sitter to stay with her when I went out I became more hardened inside.

"It isn't fair," I said to myself. "The prime of my life and it's costing me over half my paycheck to get a few free evenings." Then the guilt of feeling this way got to me and I felt like Scrooge.

Here was the woman who had nursed me through measles, mumps, chicken pox, and asthma attacks, totally shot down and I felt sorry for myself that I had to care for her. This guilt for feeling the way I did caused me to chug-a-lug even more. I loved my mother and with glass in hand I did my best to minister to her.

October 10, 1968, started off like most of my days. I was always faced with getting off to school and battling through the first few periods trying to "pull myself together" from one or eight too many.

Usually with the aid of aspirin, seltzers, and several soft drinks, by noon I could see clearly and even do a reasonable amount of teaching.

I drove home as usual that afternoon, stopping off at the liquor store for my night's supply.

I was an alcoholic.

But I was a smart alcoholic. You know, I think most alcoholics *are* smart. They have to be. That is if they want to keep the fact they drink hidden from the world. And I did want to.

I had learned to buy from different stores. Someone might suspect if I became a regular customer. I smuggled my precious cargo into my room in plastic ice chests, picnic hampers, sacks. Once I even managed to get a six-pack in my briefcase.

My mother was ill. I knew she was dying. I was the Chicken Little of the wet set. I just couldn't watch her suffer without some pain reliever for myself. She got hers at the drugstore. I got mine at the liquor store.

As I said, a consistent drinker is smart—if he thinks someone is on to him.

Once, coming home from a party, I was so bombed I could hardly see the steering wheel, not to mention the road. I had a drink on the seat next to me and was speeding home to make myself another, when through blurred eyes I saw a flashing light in the rear-view mirror.

Police!

I knew I would first have to convince them I wasn't drinking or I'd be in worse trouble than being caught for speeding. So, I put my sweater over the drink, reached above the sun visor for a bottle of breath freshener I always kept there, and quickly downed the contents.

The minute the policeman strode up to my car I started my story:

"Two guys in a white car have been following me, sir, for about two miles. I realize I was going over the speed limit, but I was scared."

I *was* scared.

"I didn't see any white car, ma'am," he said politely.

"I guess they turned off when they saw you." I was amazed at my articulation. I really could pronounce those words distinctly.

"Where do you live?" he asked.

"About five miles from here," I answered.

"Okay, tell you what. I'll forget the ticket this time, but don't be out alone this late anymore. It isn't safe. Let me pull around in front of you and I'll escort you home."

Drunker than Cooter Brown and a police escort!

I did the dumbest things. Some Friday nights I would pay a sitter to stay with Mother. Then I'd stock my front-seat cooler and head out. No destination in mind, I just drove and drank. Around midnight I started my little game.

I would stop at a pay phone, call a friend and say, "I'm drunk. I don't know where I am. But then, who cares?" Then I'd hang up and drive to another phone and call someone else with, "Guess who can't see to drive? Me. Guess who doesn't know where she is? Me."

When I look back now there is a strong resemblance to the kid with the red-handled jump rope yelling, "Look at me," and the drunk yelling the same thing.

I had stopped accepting invitations to the homes of people I knew didn't drink. I couldn't go a whole evening with no booze. So I either found a drinking buddy or sat in my room and had my own private party. Before long I had no friends so the parties in my room became more frequent.

Every afternoon after school I headed for home and mixed myself a good stiff drink. On this particular day I had two drinks and was waiting for the pleasant warm glow. It didn't come! I had a couple more and found that instead of relaxing, I began to get extremely tense, nervous, and shaky. Two more drinks. I felt worse.

I drove to the house of a friend who was a nurse and told her something was wrong. By this time I found it difficult to breathe. My heart was pounding, my vision was blurred, and it was as though some giant hand had grabbed hold of my diaphragm and wouldn't let go.

My friend called my doctor and he explained that I could be suffering from hyperventilation, the cure for which was, strangely enough, to breathe in a paper bag. I went through several bags but the condition seemed to worsen. Exhausted, I left my friend and drove the four blocks home. It was 8 P.M. I threw down six more drinks, believing soon the alcohol would surely take effect and I would calm down.

At 11 P.M. I awakened Mother. I told her I was afraid I was dying. She didn't know what to do for me but gave me aspirin, one of her sleeping pills, and told me to go lie down.

I hated to disturb her again but at 2 A.M. I had to talk to somebody.

I had tried reading, talking out loud to myself, and even tried singing. I found it difficult to focus my eyes — my head was spinning. Although I couldn't see them, crawly things were attacking me. I tried but I couldn't shake them off. Then I began to tingle in every fiber of my body. My mind wouldn't slow down. Indescribably terrifying thoughts played hopscotch in my brain. My nerves literally screamed for help.

I just knew that I was having a breakdown. I couldn't sit — stand — lie down. So I walked. It didn't really help but I had to move. So many strange things were coming alive inside me,

I guess I had to prove I could do something intentionally. So I walked.

Around 5:30 A.M. I telephoned another nurse friend and told her I needed help and within fifteen minutes she was there. I told her about the drinking right away. She went straight to the telephone and called my doctor and soon I was sitting in an emergency room. My doctor was in surgery. Two auto accidents—I was asked to wait.

An intern who took me to one of the treatment rooms said, "Now, this little shot should calm you." Maybe he said something else. I don't remember.

Nothingness. Beautiful, peaceful nothingness.

After I woke up, my own doctor was examining me, muttering that I should go home, get in bed, keep quiet and "see what happens."

Back in my own room, door shut, lying in bed—it started. The thinking, I mean. I looked around at the fifty or seventy-five books stacked on the shelves along two walls. Books piled on my desk, on the floor. All these books were mainly about philosophers, drama, poetry, or science fiction.

I smiled and thought, "There isn't a Bible anywhere." Feeling terribly tired, I wondered what was going to happen to me. My ex-roommate had talked to me about her "relationship with God" and she told me that He had kept her from taking her own life during a low period. She asked if I knew Him.

I recalled I had left her apartment after our talk and gone straight to the liquor store and I thought a lot about God that night as I drank.

"So here you are," I said aloud. "You've really botched up your life, Norman. What's left now?"

Then I remembered my mother had told me so many times that she had given me to the Lord shortly after my birth. Being born to my parents so late in their lives, she had always felt

God was going to use me in a special way. So, long ago, she had dedicated my life to Him.

I had not been blind to others' radical changes or "new lives," as they referred to them. But I knew I would never be satisfied with such a square life. The people I knew who talked about God bored me. *No,* this Christian bit was definitely not my bag. I would have to give up too much.

The day dragged by and I couldn't seem to shake the feeling of another presence in the room. I wondered about myself, grew tired of wondering, got out of bed, slipped my mother's worn Bible off her night table, and crawled back into bed.

I closed my eyes, opened the Book, put my finger on a spot on the left side of a page, opened my eyes and read the verse: "Be still, and know that I am God" (Psalms 46:10). You may believe that my hands opened to that page and my finger pointed to that verse by chance, if you wish.

Now, I had never really talked to God. Oh, I had reeled off my prayers as a child, but that day I knelt beside my bed and *I talked to God.*

"God, it's me," I began. "It's a new experience to be talking to You, but for the first time, for some reason, I know You're here."

The words kept coming and before long there was nothing in the world but God and me, and I knew He was listening to *me.*

"I've heard other people talk about how You've helped them, and now, finally, I'm asking You to help *me.* I want You to come into my heart. I don't know if I'm asking right or not, but I need You to help me. And God, if You'll take away my *desire* to drink, I'll never let You down and I'll read Your Word and learn about You. And I'll share what I learn with others. Amen."

That was the prayer. I now belonged to God and He was living inside me. I got back into bed and began to thumb eagerly through Mother's Bible. One of the verses she had underlined was: "Behold, I stand at the door, and knock: if any man hear my voice, and open the door, I will come in . . ." (Revelation 3:20).

And that's what had just happened. He had been there all those years and finally I opened up and asked Him in—into my heart—into my life.

I turned the New Testament pages like crazy, reading all the verses Mother had underlined. Another one read: ". . . if any man be in Christ, he is a new creature: old things are passed away; behold, all things are become new" (2 Corinthians 5:17).

Wow! That meant that *all* I had ever done—all my sins—were gone. I was like a new-born baby, a new creature. I *did* have a future, and if it would be anything like what I was feeling in those moments, I knew it would be fantastic.

That was it. That's how the Lord and I got together. Peter Marshall entitled his testimony, "The Tap on the Shoulder." In the light of my conversion, I think I should call mine, "Knockout With a Two-by-Four."

I lay in bed holding that Bible for a long time, then got up and went to Mother's room. She asked me what I was doing out of bed.

I said simply, "Mama, it's okay. I mean *everything*. I'm going to be fine. I just gave my life to God."

She sat motionless for what seemed like a whole minute, then took my hand, bowed her head, and in a voice that sounded as though she might cry, said, "Thank You, Lord, for answering my prayers."

Then she looked up at me. "You *are* different. I can tell. Stay close to Him, Joyce, and you will always be just this happy."

I went back to my room, called my friend who had talked

to me about God, and yelled into the phone, "It happened! I'm okay now."

She knew exactly what I meant. Christians are like that. Yes, the real ones are.

On Monday I was back at school. At the beginning of each class that day I made the same little speech. I told my classes what had happened over the weekend, what I had been, and what I hoped to be from that moment on.

My students just sat and stared back at me. How would they know how to take this kooky teacher standing up there "letting it all hang out"?

I got mixed responses. Some said nothing. Some expressed happiness for me. Others were merely shocked to learn I had been a drinker.

I had, however, this intense thing about being completely honest with everybody from that point on. *And,* I wanted them to know that alcohol had just about destroyed me. And I also wanted them to know that not the psychiatric ward of any hospital, nor A.A., nor a friend, but Jesus Christ was responsible for my change.

The next day I announced to all my classes that I was forming a Bible class in my home. The Christmas story was about all I knew about the Bible, but I wanted to learn and I wanted these kids to learn with me.

Our first meeting was no smash hit. Around my coffee table in the living room sat one boy and one girl—and me. But it was the beginning of a class which during that coming summer was going to grow to ninety-five. They called themselves "Good Guys Unlimited"—trying to be good guys through the unlimited power of Jesus Christ.

Most of the high schools in town were represented, and each week the number grew, and each week one or two came to know the Lord at the end of our Bible study.

I couldn't believe God was giving *me* the chance to share His love with them. Some real toughies came to check us out and left with God's love in their hearts.

I started out with the Apostle Paul. He was easy to identify with. He had fought God, too; then God decided He could use Paul, so He gave him the message. The kids liked Paul, and I got new enthusiasm reading and teaching about this fabulous man who loved Christ so much he walked some twelve thousand miles just to tell other people about Him.

During the first few weeks of my new life, I was told by some friends in an adult Bible class I had joined, that the honeymoon feeling wouldn't last—that I must be on guard and ready for the letdown. "It happens to all new Christians," they said.

I don't know that I'm different, or that they were wrong, but I'm more thrilled with my new life, more amazed at Christ, and much more excited about it all *now* than I was then. I know one thing for sure. I stand in far greater awe.

I've seen my surroundings with new eyes, and that has made a difference, too. I've spoken to churches, clubs, schools, and camps. Every day that goes by, I am made more aware of the need in people for a personal knowledge and awareness of Jesus Christ in their lives. Oh, they may knock it, ridicule me and others who talk about Him, but they still complain and grumble about all their problems and never seem to come up with an answer.

How can a honeymoon ever be over when two people love each other, spend time together, and both love the same things?

Not long ago I spoke to a group of some fifty or sixty college students. When I got to the part about talking with God, and answered prayer, I had to stop and say to myself, "Slow down, Billy Sunday. You're overdoing it."

If a person finds his relationship with God a bore, prayer a real task, and reading the Bible a thing he feels he *must* do, he better stop and check out a few things.

And you'll find that it won't be God who is fouled up. It will be you. And the two of you can straighten things out and you'll be back in the swing again with newfound strength and joy. "Ask, believing, and you shall receive" (*see* John 16:24).

6

No Wolf at the Door

A grain of mustard seed is pretty small, but we are told that just that much faith is very potent.

At the beginning of one summer, I didn't even have that much faith. School was out. I didn't have a summer job; didn't have the slightest idea how I was going to pay rent, utilities, buy the medicine Mother needed, or pay a full-time nurse to live in and care for her.

I must admit I got pretty depressed, but I did a lot of praying. I knew God was aware of my problems and He had told me to have faith, so I stuck it out.

After about the first three weeks I had a phone call from an evangelist based here in the city. He said he needed a receptionist, as his wife, who usually worked in this capacity, would be traveling with him a lot in the summer campaigns. Also, he wanted to do two live television programs aimed primarily at teen-agers and he wanted me to help do some of the writing.

I went for an interview and discovered this whole little crusade and youth headquarters was run strictly on faith. The evangelist paid his bills and his staff's salaries. If there was any money left over, that was his salary. Some months it was pretty slim. He had a wife and three teen-age sons to support. *And,* he was planning enthusiastically on doing two television shows which would cost well over three thousand dollars to produce.

I guess that is the closest to *seeing* faith I've ever come. He told me he couldn't pay me much, but they would love to have me on their team. I coughed and asked, "How much does this job pay?"

"Well," he said, "I guess after taxes, you would be taking home a little under one hundred dollars a month."

I hadn't lived off so little money since I worked part-time in high school. My first reaction was to chuck the whole thing, but I realized an entire office staff lived by pure faith. I knew I could, too. Furthermore, I knew God wanted me to. So I accepted the job and left that office as happy as if I'd just signed a contract for five hundred dollars a week. You know, that's the way you feel when you know you are where God wants you.

I came home and made out my month's budget. I don't think Houdini could have paid four hundred dollars' worth of bills with less than one hundred dollars a month, but I knew God could, so I threw my budget book out the window and picked up another Book. In it I read, ". . . the just shall live by faith" (Hebrews 10:38). That summer I was to live *just* on faith!

Speaking engagements started coming in like crazy. At every place I spoke, someone handed me an envelope with a love offering in it. The first month went by. No wolf at the door.

I recall my prayer about God providing money for us that summer, and I have to laugh now when I think about it. You know, God has a tremendous sense of humor! I had said, "Lord, if You'll just provide enough to pay the bills, I won't ask for one penny extra."

Funny thing, that entire summer, the finances always came out almost to the *exact* amount we needed. He'd answered my prayer again. *And* there never were any pennies left over. He remembers.

As receptionist, I opened the mail in the office. I can remember more than ten letters, addressed to me, with money in them. Some were signed by someone I didn't know. Others unsigned.

To those people I don't know, I say thank you. I wrote letters to the ones with return addresses on them, but I want to say thank you again for caring and for being so unselfish to someone who really appreciated it.

This was the best summer I have ever had. I learned that you can eat faith, drive a car on faith, and even pay rent with faith.

"I will never leave thee, nor forsake thee" (Hebrews 13:5). He really meant that.

A friend who worked at the newspaper called and asked, "Have you ever done any writing? There's an opening for a reporter and the pay isn't bad. Why don't you go for an interview?"

School was due to start again in a month and I told my friend that although I'd written a column for a teacher magazine and written for my own pleasure, I couldn't just work for a month and quit.

But that night I prayed about it and the next day I kept thinking about the long summers with no pay and all the expenses that were growing every day.

"But I'm a teacher. Why would God want me to change careers?" I thought. "Me, a reporter? I can't imagine."

The following day I decided to go for an interview, knowing I'd get the don't-call-us routine. On the drive to the newspaper I prayed, "God, if You want this change to come about in my life, then let them hire me today — no writing experience and no journalism courses to my credit."

I walked out of the paper that afternoon a reporter. Well, in the sense of job title. I had a long way to go. Mother couldn't believe or understand I was no longer a teacher.

"Are you sure you can do it?" she asked. She was scared. So was I. But I knew God had gotten that job for me and I was exactly where He wanted me. He'd taken care of many biggies in my life. I knew He could handle this one.

I've been with the paper enough years to have written thousands of stories. I've met some truly beautiful people and made some lasting friends. My note pad, pen, and camera have carried me not only all over Alabama but to other states and even out of the country. To me, my job is exciting, challenging, and rewarding. I love every phase of it. I would probably still be teaching except for the fact that God wanted me at that newspaper.

The other day someone said to me, "This salvation thing you're always talking about. I don't like to hear people talk about being saved and loving everybody. I think religion is a personal thing."

I agree. Salvation is a *personal* thing. Christ came to earth and died for each one of us *personally,* so that *personally* we would be able to accept Him and have our own *personal* Saviour and *personal* relationship.

However, what this person really meant was not *personal* but *secret.*

If the disciples had kept to themselves what they had seen and heard, if Paul had gotten up from that Damascus road and looked heavenward and merely said, "Thanks for saving *me,*

Lord," and kept it to himself, if the writers of the New Testament had written all their inspired words down and then burned them because they were too *personal* — there wouldn't be any church today.

And I wouldn't know this Christ who unbelievably gave *me* new life. And neither would you.

Besides all this, Christ Himself commanded us to "Go ye therefore, and teach . . ." (Matthew 28:19). He didn't mean to hide that joy behind any door. It meant just what He said, "Go and teach . . . ."

You live forever with Christ by faith and by believing and accepting the fact that Jesus Christ died and rose for you. You thank Him for dying so that you won't ever have to die. You invite Him to take complete control of your life because you know He's out of that tomb.

How can you keep quiet about the thrill you possess, the joy that is yours, and the knowledge that there is a world out there searching for something?

I love that song, "Go Tell It on the Mountain." Do you ever feel so full of God's love you want to do just that? I do!

And I'm the one who thought I'd have to give up so much if I became a Christian. If I'd only known.

7

Christian Watchers

As the weeks of my new life rolled into months, I began to wonder about attitude. I mean in the sense of what my attitude toward Christ really was, about people's attitudes toward me, and my attitude toward them.

I knew what my attitude toward Christ was. He had total control of my life and I exercised the "hands off" method as much as I could. I knew beyond any doubts that I had found life's Answer. It was Jesus Christ. I loved Him and wanted to give of myself to others and love them.

But what about others' attitudes toward me? Oh, I don't mean as a person, but as a Christian. After all, I was on His team now. I represented Him, spoke openly for Him, so people pretty much knew where I stood.

I wanted desperately to be so God-centered that others would see something different about me, that they would respond and be lured to *like* that difference so that I would have the opportunity to tell them who had made the difference.

So, being a baby Christian, I watched others—others I

thought more mature Christians. Someone once said the world is full of Christian watchers. I believe it.

I would come into contact with Christians in meetings and in church, and they seemed so enthusiastic about Christ. When I would see them elsewhere, they seemed to sing a different tune. A sort of "I'll-Never-Forget-What's-His-Name" melody instead of "To Know Him Is to Love Him."

I believe it was at this point that I fully realized the responsibility of calling oneself *Christian*. It was then that I became aware of how difficult it was going to be being a consistent follower of Christ. At least for me, anyway. But, it was also at this point that I discovered the marvelous, comforting verse, "I can do all things through Christ which strengtheneth me" (Philippians 4:13). People are constantly looking for flaws in a Christian. They have to, you see, or their arguments about hypocrites are wiped out.

I recall telling a friend in a Bible class something in confidence. It was of no great consequence, but I had asked this friend to pray about it and not to tell anyone else. I trusted her and took great stock in her prayers.

By noon the next day I had heard my prayer request two times from other friends!

James has a lot to say about the tongue and how, although it is so small, it can be very lethal. I learned one thing, however. ". . . let your requests be made known unto *God*" and "trust in the Lord" (Philippians 4:6, 2:24).

Another lesson I learned was, if I have to wear a bumper sticker on my car for people to know I am a Christian, I'm failing.

If being sure I don't miss a Sunday in church is my proof I am a Christian, I'm failing.

No, it must come from within me and I must exude that Man so much that my conversation and my actions will become living proof of His existence in me. God needs ambassadors and I surely would like to be a good one.

But then I came to another rather startling realization. And this comes from much prayer and a great deal of thought.

I spoke earlier about Christian watchers. I work in the so-called secular world and I know how a great majority of people feel about Christianity. Generally, they feel it has *no* place outside the walls of the church.

I began to feel a wad of frustration building up within me. If a Christian watcher eyed me for long he'd be very disillusioned. I said and did things I knew weren't right.

Then I salved my mind by saying, "Well, I'm only human."

That is when it hit me. That's the point in time when things began to fit together.

Non-Christians expect nothing less than perfection from a professing Christian. And because I was well aware that I was falling far short of this, I became confused and extremely concerned as to how to conduct myself.

Then I said that sentence again. Only this time out loud. "I'm only human."

That's when I knew my attitude about being a Christian had been all wrong. Because I *was* human, I could *never* attain perfection, nor come anywhere close to it. And I began to settle down into the knowledge that although Jesus Christ was indeed living in me, I could never be perfect. *Never.*

Christians sometimes flippantly use the term, "To be like Jesus," and non-Christians expect just that. From us they expect the strength of Jesus—the courage of Jesus—the honesty of Jesus—yes, even His perfection.

And of course, they are disappointed because the fact remains we *are* humans and only rarely are we even able to show hints of any of these qualities in our lives. Many Christians need to face up to this.

We spout all this "religious jargon" we've heard, but our actions and responses are totally opposite to what we say.

I heard a non-Christian say the other day (I learn so much about Christians from non-Christians), "That guy on the second floor really makes me laugh. He won't come to any of the parties we give here because we usually serve liquor. Somebody tells a joke and he gets up and leaves. But you ought to see how he cheated on his income tax this year. And gossip? He's the best! See, Christians are just two-faced. At least I'm honest."

There is nothing wrong with trying to be *like* Jesus. But too many of us forget He was God's Son—perfect. He was born perfect and He died perfect. No sin breaks that statement.

I'm His child but I'm His human child and He knows I couldn't be perfect if I locked myself in my room and had no contact whatsoever with the outside world. Before five minutes was up, I'd botch everything and *think* something I shouldn't.

So I stopped right then and there trying to "act like a Christian" and started being *me* with all my faults and frailties.

When Christ came into my life He hadn't destroyed my personality. I hope He's refined and shaped it up, but basically I had to be me. Me, getting instructions from my Father.

Things changed after that. I didn't walk around like "Miss Pious" anymore. I let my non-Christian friends know there had been a radical change in my life, but I also let them know I was still me. The same me they could laugh and joke with. The same me they could invite to their homes, serve cocktails, and not be made uncomfortable by my presence. It was the same me, but they saw the difference. I stopped believing I had attained perfection with salvation and just loved them. I didn't condone. But I didn't condemn, either. "I'm only human."

I work with a very attractive young woman, or at least we work in the same building. When I first met her I must admit I didn't like her very much. I realized at the time I should not feel this way, but my "humanness" was overactive and I had a very poor concept of her.

I thought she was cold, a snob, unfeeling, and totally lacking in humor. And one day when I was told I would have to work with her on an assignment, I looked on it as a real task that I would simply have to endure.

The assignment was of a week's duration, and that meant every day for seven days I would have to come in contact with her.

As the days began to pass, I felt my animosity toward her start to dwindle. I watched her go about her work and I developed a genuine respect for the manner in which she worked. She was well-organized, punctual, and talked to me in a pleasant way.

One afternoon we were taking a break and over a soft drink I got a close-up look at this person. I saw someone very unhappy and lonely. And I felt ashamed of the things I had thought.

I've known her for over a year now and I consider her special. I keep telling her God loves her and so do I and I think she's beginning to believe this.

Also, I believe she knows I care and would walk the second mile, or the third—even the tenth, if she needed me to.

One evening on the phone she said, "Maybe God can help me." He's a part of her vocabulary. He will soon be a vital part of her life.

God's love cannot be seen on this earth unless we show it. So because my dear friend knows I love her, so must she surely know it is God inside loving her through me.

It didn't hurt to reach out to her. It did wonders for me, personally. It thrills me so much to hear her laugh. And of late, she's been doing a lot more of it.

She brought me a New Testament from a recent trip to New York. Although I have four or five other Bibles, this New Testament holds great meaning for me and I carry it with me everywhere.

I cannot believe I haven't always liked her. Because of God I feel I've known her for years. That's how He works in lives. When two people make contact on God's wavelength, there is a bond set that can never be broken. Because He *first* loved *me,* He has given me the desire to love *others.*

God loved my friend before I did but she needed to *see* His love in action and that's where we come in. If you feel that occupying a pew on Sundays, singing hymns louder than the fellow next to you, and having a prayer group meet at your home every so often pacifies God, you're wrong. Paul said without *love* we are nothing.

I know a woman who does all the above, but if she has any sincere love in her for people outside her circle of church friends, it doesn't show. She is critical and points the verbal finger every chance she gets.

The sooner we understand with our *hearts* (many know and believe with their heads) that Jesus came to us, died for us, and rose again for us—*because He loved us,* the sooner we will be able to love the ones around us who need love the most. Perhaps we need to stop trying to "be *like* Jesus" and just let Him "be Himself" through us.

I hope my friend can see Jesus despite my humanness. If He can overcome death, I know He can overcome me and love through me.

The guy with the trash mouth who works upstairs looks different to me. I feel sorry that he doesn't know Christ. Also,

I've figured out he must *really* be interested because he knocks Christianity a lot and spends a great deal of time talking about God not existing. It is almost as though I expect him any day to come up with, "I'm an atheist. God knows I'm an atheist!"

I only pray God will use me *and* all my humanness as an instrument to at least cause others to *question* the differences in my life. In so questioning them, they are closer than they know to understanding what Jesus meant when He said, ". . . seek, and ye shall find" (Luke 11:9).

I thought I had finished this chapter but found I hadn't. I took a break before going on and am awfully glad I did.

My friend from work called and invited me to dinner with her, Freita Fuller (Miss Alabama), and her parents. It was the night before the Auburn-Tennessee football game and every restaurant in town was overflowing.

After much searching we found a place that had a table for the five of us. We were seated at a table in the center of the room and surrounded by excited football fans.

After we had finished eating, I assumed we would leave as Freita had a date and was to call him when we got through with dinner.

I really can't remember how the conversation got around to God, but it did. The Fullers are fine examples of Christians who love and love and give so much of themselves. Mr. Fuller is in the automobile business but he takes care of God's business first.

I believe I asked Freita how a recent appearance at a youth rally in Kentucky (where she had spoken) had gone. As she began to share with me I saw the Fullers and my friend engaged in a lively conversation at the other end of the table. I had no idea what they were discussing. Then I heard the word "God" about every other sentence and Freita and I stopped our talk and listened.

How can you adequately describe a thrill? How can you give wordage to emotion?

There at the other end of the table sat my friend, gesturing and talking excitedly about *God* and the closeness she felt for Him. We sat there for two hours. I looked around the room and the irony of it all caused me to smile. There we were, surrounded by drinking, loud football fans speculating on the game to come, and our conversation was of God and His love and reality to each of us.

We took Freita and her parents back to their hotel and my friend and I went to the parking lot to get our cars. I can't say it was raining because it was a deluge. It was pouring, lightning bolts broke the darkness of the sky, and the wind was blowing hard.

My friend got in her car and with rain beating down on my body, I stuck my head in the car and said, "What a thrill tonight was! You really opened up and God *is* a part of you. He's very real and tonight it showed."

She just smiled and agreed it had been a good evening. Then she added, "It all is faith, Joyce. Not works. Just faith. I *do* believe."

I could have walked the three miles home in the rain! Already soaked to the skin, nothing mattered except that my friend had shared her love and relationship with Jesus Christ.

Cold, unfeeling, a snob—all presumptions wiped away. She is a child of God's and it showed on her face in the car while the lightning furnished the illumination.

I can thank God for answered prayer—for rain—for lightning—thunder—and a person who at last openly admitted God lives within her.

8

Now I Lay Me Down

Prayer. Now that's something no Christian can get along without. Not a one-a-day capsule prayer, but a continual conversation with God every moment of the day. Even *thinking* about God is praying.

Henry Drummond said in regard to prayer, "Ten minutes . . . ay, two minutes if it be face to face, and heart to heart, will make the whole day different." Now, he's speaking in terms of carrying on an intelligent conversation with God. Not these dull, Now-I-lay-me-down-to-sleep-type prayers while lying in bed. This kind of prayer usually ends with "Now I lay me down!"

To know Him *is* to love Him—*more*. The best way to know a friend is to spend time with him, talk to him, share your thoughts and feelings with him, even cry on his shoulder if you feel like it.

That's the way it is with the Lord and me. I drive down the highway to an assignment and I pray. I feel sure my fellow highway travelers think I'm singing along with the radio. But I'm talking to God.

For me, at least, it is the best time to talk to Him. It is quiet, I'm alone, and I usually have a good hour or two to spend with Him.

I recall one trip. I prayed all the way about Mother. She was in the hospital and going through a rough time. She was taking some drugs which had caused her to have hallucinations— seeing things that weren't there, terror in her face, afraid of everybody who came near her, including me.

I had left her in this state the night before. I had to do my interview, but I was deeply concerned about her, wondering if she would pull out of this new horror. The doctor said he didn't think he would take her off the drug because it might regress her terminal illness.

When I got to my interview, I called the hospital. The woman in the next bed answered the phone. I asked, "How is everything?"

She responded with, "Your mother wants to talk to you."

Mother came on the line and I knew by the tone of her voice that God had been listening because she said, "How are you? I feel so much better today and the doctor told me this morning he had stopped that new drug."

On the way back to the office I sang!

God answers prayer. I know. He's answered too many of mine and I've seen Him answer friends' prayers.

I believe the sweetest, most meaningful prayer I have yet to hear was uttered by a teen-age boy at a Good Guys' Bible Study. The boy's older sister, a Christian of two months, insisted that he come that particular night. He laughed and in his own words replied, "Ain't *no* way."

She informed him we always had four or five cheerleaders there, so he agreed to come—once. Even so, she told me, he had threatened to get out of the car at every stoplight en route.

I was in the kitchen when they arrived and the girl walked up to me and said, "My brother is here tonight."

We had been praying for him a long time, so this in itself was an answer.

All the kids sat in a big circle in my living room. That night it was overflowing. It just so happened that this boy could find no other spot but the only empty space on the carpet — right in front of me. He sat on the floor and looked up at me like, "Okay, chick, let's get this over with."

Talk about feeling inadequate. I mean like I wished for Billy Graham. Here sat this seventeen-year-old, belligerent as everything, staring right at me. I had the feeling I was fishing, had a big one on the line, and had suddenly forgotten how to reel.

Well, up went a miniature prayer and I started in to tell about Paul being imprisoned, the earthquake coming, and everybody in the jail carrying on while he sang songs of praise.

At the end of the study, I tried to show how Christians have nothing to fear. They can sing in the face of disaster because they know God is with them. I guess I said more, but I can't remember now exactly what.

As usual, we had prayer time and we went around the circle. I had told the kids if they didn't want to pray to merely say, "I pass," and the next one would pick it up. (By the way, the first two or three weeks of our Bible studies sounded like a card game, but before long no one passed anymore.)

It came the young man's turn and he said, "I pass," as I'd fully expected. I closed with prayer and we had refreshments.

I was in the kitchen serving when this tall, dark-haired boy tapped me on the arm and asked, "Could I talk to you outside for a minute?"

On the way to the front porch, I told David, a friend who helped me with the Bible class, to come, too. He got the boy's sister's attention, so all four of us stood on the porch in near darkness.

"I listened to those prayers in there," the young man said,

"and I didn't know other kids had some of the same problems I have. They told all their sins right out loud. They all seem so happy. How do I get this?"

I was remembering how to reel.

David explained how one becomes a child of God and then asked if he wanted to wait until next week to make any definite decision.

"No," he quickly answered. "I want it now."

So David started to pray, when the boy suddenly broke in with his own prayer. I looked up and could see tears trickling down his cheeks. There stood the four of us, all holding hands and listening to somebody really *talking* to God. He asked Him to come into his heart and make him new. He must have prayed for five minutes.

Afterward, we went back in the house and I announced we had a new "Good Guy." Everybody swarmed him and told him how thrilled they were.

The last time I saw this boy, he was standing on a platform sharing God's love with others.

Yes, God answers prayer and I am more convinced every day that talking things over with a God who responds is the most exciting and rewarding thing in the world.

Before leaving this beautiful subject of prayer, there's another story. I knew God was right there with me.

It had been a little over a year since I had had a drink. I was asked to cover a fashion show. Cocktails preceded the showing. When asked by the bartender what I wanted to drink, I replied, "Ginger ale." Almost in unison, the people around me said, "What's wrong with you? You don't drink? Why?"

It has really amazed me about this drinking thing. If you *take* a drink, no one ever asks, "Why?" Yet, if you refuse, they assume you're some kind of nut. "You mean you don't drink? What's wrong with you?"

Maybe people don't like to drink alone. I don't know. But I *do* know they can be very insistent. One fellow kept coming up to me all evening saying, "You still drinking ginger ale? You don't know what you're missing." If he only knew!

It wasn't until I was home later that night that it hit me what I had experienced. I had spent an entire evening with people who were almost all drinking and the thought of my drinking never entered my mind.

Then I remembered my first prayer, "God, take away the *desire.*" That is exactly what He had done.

And God had given me a love and concern for the people in that party who *were* drinking. The only feeling I can recall is wondering how the two or three drunks in the crowd would get home and wishing people would learn moderation.

I saw a good friend there and although she wasn't "knee-walkin' " she was feeling no pain.

Carol (a name I'll use to protect my friend) has no apparent, obvious reason to drink as much as she does. But I understand this kind of reasoning. People used to think the same about me. Maybe it's something ugly inside her that alcohol deadens.

Whatever her reason, or reasons, Carol is well on her way to becoming an alcoholic. *And,* typically, she would be the last person to admit it.

"I can handle my liquor," she says, pouring another drink.

She cannot go to a party and enjoy herself unless she's had a couple before going and then she drinks throughout the evening. A fun time to her is "a few friends and lots of booze." I know the feeling. I've been there and that's why I ache so for Carol.

She protests too much, also. To hear her talk, only the "in" people and the "beautiful" people drink. I've never heard her ask someone to stop by her home for a cup of coffee. It's *always* for a drink. I wish she really knew some of the beautiful people I know. Sure, they have vices like all of us, but they don't have to escape into a martini to enjoy life.

We hear so much talk about the harmful effects of drugs on our bodies. But it's almost common and mind-staggering knowledge that an excess of alcohol is as much of a destroyer of the human race as narcotics.

When Carol is sober she usually calls me and almost always says, "Joyce, I want to quit drinking. After 5 P.M. I'm just a vegetable. Help me."

How can I help her? Not by preaching or giving her "my story." I believe as a Christian the only way I can help her is to love her — to outwardly show love for her when she has none for herself.

And to pray for her. I don't give up on people anymore. I still vividly remember my own personal experience with Christ and I know He doesn't give up either.

Other desires have come to take the place of the one God removed. But, they are good, meaningful desires because they are God-motivated.

There is such a difference in desires. If there is any doubt in your mind about which are yours and which are God's, get it straight. You'll never be happy until you do.

Perhaps another word for desire is passion. Regardless, man is created so that he can feel strongly about things. He desires things. He wants things. He has a *passion* for things. And unless God is doing the driving, this part of man can get him into a lot of trouble.

When I asked God to remove the desire for alcohol, He didn't leave any void. For one reason, the devil loves to work with voids. When there is an empty spot in man, it is a perfect setup for Satan to appear and try to fill that empty space.

That red man is so subtle, he can convince you that you are right, even when you know you are not.

As an example, I no longer had the desire to drink. But, I began to get an unhealthy attitude about people who did. I really was hard on them. I actually condemned them. Oh, not overtly, but I thought about it a lot. I hadn't as yet learned much tolerance and I was in no position to point any finger at anybody who bent the old elbow. God is love and I had to work on this.

The idea ran around in my head for several days. I decided to really pray about it. Now see, the devil just doesn't like you to talk things over with God, because he knows God enlightens.

After praying about it, I didn't think about it so much, but I was still looking for my answer. "For ye have need of patience" (Hebrews 10:36).

One afternoon a neighbor dropped in holding a drink in her hand. After a half-hour's talk she suddenly jumped to her feet and said, "Oh, I'm sorry. I forgot, you don't drink. I shouldn't have brought this glass in here."

If I was ever going to show anybody that Christ's way is the *only* way and that God loves, I certainly couldn't do it by giving my friend a lengthy, pious lecture on temperance.

I asked her to sit down again and told her not to worry about me.

The thing that amazed me was that this woman calmed down, began to open up to me, and we had a wonderful afternoon together. We talked about alcohol but she wasn't uncomfortable. Christians should never cause others to feel uncomfortable or out of place. This woman felt I loved her despite the fact we had different views on some things. We need to realize that *differences* must not separate us from people. Christians, of all people, should be able to overlook them and love the person. Christ did.

I had known this person for over a year and that one afternoon made us good friends.

The kindest, most understanding Person who ever lived was Jesus. That knowledge brought me to a great awakening about tolerance.

In regard to desires, I even said in the preceding paragraphs another word was passion. I think I know of another word, too — *enthusiasm.*

It seems as I stand off and look at my life now, that this is what God has overendowed me with — enthusiasm.

Now since drink was my showy problem, you probably think I really hit hard on this one topic. Not so. I talk about it only in relation to its separating me from serving God. What I'm really enthusiastic about is Christian *living.* When I get up to speak to young people or adults, I really get fired up and enthusiastic on this topic.

If you've ever stood behind a rostrum and addressed a group of people, you know what I'm talking about. People, for the most part, are cold, expressionless — just sitting there. But the more I talk about God, His fantastic love, His marvelous life, the new exciting life He offers everyone, the more excited I become. There sits my audience, staring back as if to say, "What on earth is she talking about? Why all the enthusiasm? She's really gung-ho."

First of all, I'm *talking about Christ.* You all remember Him, now don't you? He's the Man you read about in Sunday school as a child — the One who died on a cross. Most people put a *period* at the end of this last sentence. At least that's the way they look.

He died on a cross. YES. Period. But I'm telling you He didn't *stay* on that cross or in that tomb. He lives! I know. Just look at me. Remember what I was like? Then I realize they don't know. They didn't know me then.

Why all the enthusiasm? Because *I* remember what I was like and *I* *know* that now there is no comparison. Oh, I'm not Rebecca of Sunnybrook Farm by a long shot, but I *am* a child of God, trying to serve Him and receiving goodness from Him every day. When I see those blank stares, I wonder if they know the happiness God offers. They don't look as if they do. So, I try to impart to them, as best I can, how I feel about God. YES, I get enthusiastic.

It really excites me when I think God sent His only Son for *me*. Someone did a parody on the Hallmark card slogan and I think it fits what I'm talking about very well: GOD: HE CARED ENOUGH TO SEND THE VERY BEST.

I realized the other day sitting on a platform before a talk to a group of college kids, that Christianity is the *only* message that *tells it like it was, like it is, and like it will be.*

Someone said to me the other day, "I'm as religious and as good as anyone. I go to church. What else am I expected to do?" I became curious to know what Mr. Webster's book had to say about the word "religious." I personally do not like the word, or what my mind conjures up when I hear it. The dictionary defines "religious" as "scrupulously faithful or conscientious." Does this sound like our pious friend?

But, in the light of what else the fellow had to say, I believe two of Mr. Webster's words would be more appropriate. One is "religionism." It is defined as "pretense of religion." Another is "religiosity," meaning, "religious, especially when affected." With these two new words, I would venture to say our man has a good case of *religionism.* He pretends he has feelings about God, when in actuality he has no real, genuine, deep-rooted feelings or emotions at all.

I recall as a youngster, Ralph and I used to play games—

pretending we were someone other than ourselves. I was always yelling, "Play like I'm Jane and you're Tarzan." Play like — not *being,* but *pretending* to be.

There was most assuredly no pretense in Christ's life. He was never, nor did He *pretend* to be anything other than who He was — the Son of God. Despite harassment, persecution, and eventual death, He never once sidestepped His identity or His reason for visiting our planet.

Yet people, not just this one man, pretend to be religious and like the actors or actresses they are, they fool many people. But they don't fool God. He knows what we think *before* we think it, and "as he thinketh in his heart, so is he" (Proverbs 23:7).

Who are you? Do you know? God does.

Going to church, even teaching a Sunday-school class or Bible study, will never take the place of the Holy Spirit of God living within you. After awhile, you won't even be able to fool people. The real down-to-earth, God-geared Christian will spot you.

Do you know what will give you away first? Your face. There is just something different about the face of a happy, born-again God-child. There's a special loving, outgoing quality that lets people know you care because God cares.

Your conversation will give the next hint. Christians, lovers of God, talk about Him. They have real caring and they talk about Christ and the need for Him in our world. Their faces light up when they talk about a new follower or an answered prayer.

Finally, and I believe the most important thing that will bring out your true colors, is your "fruit." ". . . by their fruits ye shall know them" (Matthew 7:20). Do you bring forth fruit? Do you ache for the unhappy folks around you? Do you have compassion for them?

Every time you hear the Lord's name taken in vain, do you

hurt? Do you defend the Man who died for you? Some people would put up the old fists if anyone ridiculed a friend or a member of their family, but can sit placidly by and hear the mighty loving God mocked, ridiculed, and dragged in the dirt — and remain unmoved.

I don't think you should raise your fists, or drag out your soap box, but God gave pretty explicit instructions on what you *could* do. *And,* He said these words while He was nailed to a cross. He aimed them at the very ones who had put Him there. "Father, forgive them; for they know not what they do" (Luke 23:34). A lot of us need to work on our "forgivers."

So, that means to love *them* enough to forgive them their blasphemous words, and to love *Christ* enough to share what you know about Him.

"I go to church. What else am I expected to do?"

Whatever I do for Christ is so pitifully small and insignificant in the light of what He did for me. What are you expected to do? Follow Him. Live for Him. Love Him.

Don't play Christian. More harm is done by toy Christians than this world dreams of. A Christian watcher may be watching you. Of all people, he's the best at spotting a phony.

In thinking about toy Christians and spotting phonies, I remembered an assignment I had that brought home to me that it really is difficult to maintain a consistent disguise of what and who we really are.

The circus was coming to town. I racked my brain thinking of an angle to write about. One of our reporters was going to ride an elephant from the train station to the auditorium. I decided I would like to know how it felt to be a clown. So I called the public-relations man for the circus and he gladly consented to my appearing at the opening performance as a guest clown.

I went in looking like me, but one hour later the mirror reflected the funniest face I'd ever seen. *I* was a clown and in

the striped green and white shirt and plaid baggy pants, I felt
like one. I had a couple of little tricks to perform with the
regular clowns and then was told to "just have fun."

I thought back to circuses with my father and I guess he'd
have laughed at me that day, too. For weeks following every
circus, my backyard was a one-ring affair. The other kids
could be anything they wanted, but I was always a clown.

So that afternoon was special to me and when the lights went
out, a spotlight illumined the ringmaster and he announced,
"Ringling Brothers—Barnum and Bailey Circus proudly
presents 'The Greatest Show On Earth,'" and I thought I
would melt and run out the legs of my baggy pants. I even
admit to a fleeting thought of leaving my job and joining the
circus. This was excitement and I was right in the middle of it!

All the clowns ran into the arena and we jumped, skipped,
turned summersaults, and the crowd laughed. This was one
assignment when I didn't need my note pad. The story was
being written in my head.

During the last intermission I was told I could go out front
and watch the remainder of the show. In a way I was glad.
Being a clown is hard work and I was thoroughly exhausted.

I had made sure my four-year-old godson, Jon, had gotten a
ticket and earlier in the show had spotted him sitting wide-eyed
in the front row. With makeup and costume still on I started
walking across the sawdust to where he was sitting. I was a bit
afraid he would be frightened by the clown heading in his
direction. Halfway to him the other children in the area began
pointing at me, laughing and giggling. Then I saw Jon spot me.
He stood up, smiled, waved, and in a voice loud enough for
half the audience to hear, yelled, "Hi, Aunt Joyce!"

I thought I'd really pulled a sneak on the kid. All the time
he knew who I was! I sat down next to him and in a very low-
keyed voice asked, "How about some of your popcorn, kid?"

I didn't see much of the remainder of the show. A good

lesson had been brought home to me that afternoon. No matter what we do or what our disguises, people usually see right through us.

I thought of all the people I know who play the clown every day, thinking no one knows what's happening behind the mask. And right there in that circus a verse of Scripture came to me: "The fool hath said in his heart, There is no God" (Psalms 14:1).

That's what part a clown plays—a fool. But underneath the greasepaint and funny clothes are real people. They, at least, can remove the exterior.

And I thought of a discussion I had with a young man who, although working on his master's degree and maintaining an *A* grade average, had told me, "I like you. You taught me in school and I have much respect for you. But you have lost your head over this 'God thing.' There is no God. Of this I am convinced."

With all this boy's intellect, he has missed the point for living, and according to God's Word, he is a fool. God is not vague. His signs are all around us.

Then I thought of another verse, "We are fools for Christ's sake, but ye are wise in Christ" (1 Corinthians 4:10). I'm sure I look the fool to this boy who "doth protest too much" that there is no God. Since talk is useless with him, I now just pray that the God he denies verbally will one day make Himself real to this young man. He's not the type to heckle or ridicule so that is why I am encouraged that he calls at least once a week and consistently asks, "Still believe there is a God?"

My answer is always the same—"More than ever."

It's funny that I thought of all this in the middle of a circus. Jon was the one who triggered the thinking and someday when he's older I'll thank him.

I'm still amazed that no matter where I am—there is God.

9

My Mother

Mother and I became the best of friends during her stay with me in Birmingham. She never bugged me about where I was going or when I'd be back. I know she felt awful the majority of the time but every time I'd say, "Want to go for a drive?" she'd perk up, put on some lipstick, and off we'd go.

I learned more about my mother during those years — what she was like as a child growing up in the flatlands of West Texas. She'd sit propped up in bed and forget her pain as she told of going to square dances with her brothers in a horse-drawn buggy. "I always carried a hatpin with me in case a fellow got fresh," she'd laugh.

I got to know her as a person and her humor knocked me out. I'd get dressed to go somewhere and walk in her room and ask how I looked. She'd wink and say, "You don't look too bad, hon."

Every article in the paper with my by-line on it she cut out and put in a box. Then when the only friend she'd been able to make in Birmingham, Mrs. Emma Reed, came to visit, she'd get out that box of clippings and show her every one. Bless Mrs. Reed. She must have looked at those things hundreds of times.

On a Christmas day, Mother went to the hospital for the last time. I believe she knew she wouldn't be coming back. Before the ambulance came she had me help her walk around the apartment and she touched everything. "Don't forget to water my plants," was the last sentence she said when she saw the ambulance pull up in front.

Her doctor knew the outlook was grim. Mother and he had become good friends during her stay. I cannot sing his praises loudly enough. Knowing she had terminal cancer, he just gave her enough pain-killers to keep her comfortable. He didn't subject her to tests, new experiments, or drugs. Her weekly visits to his office were farces, really. He'd check her blood pressure, do a simple examination, and then take her into his office and just visit with her. I believe the fact he didn't use her as a guinea pig made her think she wasn't as ill as she was. As the cancer began to destroy vertebrae and the pain got pretty fierce, he'd just say, "Could be arthritis." That pacified her.

But this last hospital trip was different. Her pain had gotten so bad he decided he would at last try a new drug to see if it would help. It didn't, and when he called me out in the hall one afternoon and said, "Joyce, I've done all I can. She's not responding. I think you should fly her back to Texas. It won't be long now," he had tears in his eyes.

So, after a month's stay in the hospital, Mother and I flew to Fort Worth. I firmly believe God gave us that two-hour flight. She sat next to the window and it was a beautiful day for flying. The sun sparkled off the wings and the clouds were big and white in contrast to the deep blue of the sky. Just before we landed, she took my hand and said, "Honey, I wish we could just keep flying, going higher and higher. I feel God today and I'm ready to keep climbing until I get to Him."

Because she now required full-time medical care, my brother and I put her in a nursing home. She wasn't too happy with this but she was back in Texas and that did make her happy.

But her doctor was right. It wasn't long and one Wednesday night at 7:30, my sweet mother slipped away to be with God.

There were no tears. Her little tired body just stopped functioning, and she was with God.

We had the funeral services on my birthday. Somehow it seemed fitting that this should be the day for such an event. I never had such a birthday gift before — a day filled with memories I had forgotten — the family together, talking of Mother and what she had meant to each of us.

I could not express then, nor can I now, what her life meant and means to me. I miss her terribly. God alone knows how much. But up to the very end she never stopped being a "high place" to me.

She was small, but she was strong, with an almost superhuman strength the doctors couldn't understand. One doctor in particular used the term *fighter*. I had three red roses sent to the church with a card attached that read: "I have fought the good fight; I have finished the course; I have kept the faith."

That was eulogy enough. That verse said it all. Because *she* had kept the faith, she strengthened and encouraged me to. Because *she* fought a good fight, she spurred me on when I felt low.

Without God, I could never have lived through the days that preceded her death, nor the time afterward. I had been praying for strength when the time came and God poured it out. You see, He was acquainted with grief and was a Man of sorrows, so He knew my heart and how I felt.

Mother loved her children — my two older brothers and me.

Her last words were that we love each other and that we love and follow God.

She left behind a legacy worth more than any bank could hold. She left me, personally, a picture etched indelibly on my memory of her smile and her love.

During our last months together, her prayers were more and more of commitment. She wanted her health back and never stopped praying, "Lord, heal my body, but if it isn't Thy will . . . ."

I'm thankful and grateful to God that I had a Christian mother. I hope I told her often enough how I felt, but somehow I feel she knew.

Edna St. Vincent Millay said it: "Where she once was, there is a hole in the world."

But she is with God and so am I. So, we're still together.

10

I Am With You Always

Before Mother died, a friend asked me to go to Japan as a summer missionary. My first thought, in all honesty, was, "Why should I?"

"There really is a need in a small Christian mission over there and they want someone to teach and relieve the missionary's wife of some of her duties for the summer. You're qualified to teach, so why not apply?" he asked.

I had been out of teaching a year at this point and was a writer. "Why, I couldn't possibly teach again," I thought— and a lot of other excuses like not being able to get off from the newspaper for three months!

Also, could I leave Mother?

I didn't think these were excuses; just valid reasons why I could not go.

But at my friend's insistence, I wrote TEAM, The Evangelical Alliance Mission, and applied. Forms were sent back and forth and several phone calls came from TEAM headquarters.

Then, in late April, the letter came. I had been selected to go to the town of Takamatsu and work for the summer. I had prayed about this ever since I first applied, always saying, "God, You know the obstacles. But, if You want me to go, I'm ready. If I'm not willing, make me willing to be willing."

A week later my mom passed away. Now no home ties held me back. It was a matter of talking to the newspaper and asking for time off.

Before I was to leave, optimistic as I by then had become, I went for a general medical checkup. Heart, lungs — I had the normal number of each and they were okay.

Then came the more intensive examination and sitting in my doctor's office afterward, waiting for him to come in and fill out the necessary medical forms, I was completely unaware of a great change about to take place in my life.

The doctor came in, sat down behind his desk. I'm a bit afraid of doctors who don't smile, but even more leery of those who smile a lot. My doctor's smile was a yard wide.

"I know about this Japan trip, and I feel like a dog," he said, "but I've got to schedule you for surgery. You have an extremely enlarged right ovary and I suspect a growth. I'm sorry; I know you had counted on the trip."

"Couldn't I go after the operation?"

"No. I want to wait three weeks to operate in order to build up your blood and get some extra weight on you. That would leave only three weeks before you're scheduled to go. It can't be done."

I went home bogged down with iron pills and a crazy mixed-up mind. I couldn't believe God would take me this far and then close the door.

But three weeks later I entered the hospital as mentally prepared as I could be for the operation. I really wasn't too afraid.

Not because I was so big and brave, but because all my friends had brainwashed me by saying, "There's nothing to it. You won't know a thing."

Concerning the latter statement, they were right. I was out for two days. But there *was* something to it. When I could comprehend things, my doctor informed me that he had performed a complete hysterectomy. He had found endometrioses growing on vital organs in my body. My modest doctor took no credit for lifesaving, but I certainly sent a lot of thank You prayers up to God.

In the days that followed, I lay in the hospital bed and answers began to heal along with the incision.

My mother had died on May 1. I had been kept from going to Japan. I had had major surgery on May 28 – surgery that revealed a serious future ahead for me physically, if it had not been performed when it had.

In the four weeks at home in which I recuperated, I had lots of time to think and God and I enjoyed many beautiful sessions.

I had many visitors who dropped in during this period to bring me a cake, cookies, soup, or books to read.

One friend was sitting on my sofa one afternoon and she looked at me very intently and said, "Joyce, I really don't know how you've done it."

"Done what?" I asked.

"Well," she said, "your mother's illness drained you emotionally and physically, I know. You've lost about twenty-five pounds. She died in May and you had surgery twenty-seven days later. No family was with you and yet you look like the happiest person in the world."

After she left I began to think about what she had said. To be perfectly honest, my first thought was, "You know, she's right. That wasn't exactly the merry month of May for me. I wonder why God let everything happen during this one month." (I was beginning to feel like Job!)

Then I thought again and realized that not one time during May had I questioned God or really even thought much about the events of those days. It all boiled down to the fact I had been so close to Him since my conversion, had complete and abandoned trust in Him, and believed that whatever course my life took was okay—simply because God was there. I had no cause to question or dwell on "whys."

When Christ came into my life I went all the way with Him. I believed Him when I read in my Bible, "I will never leave you nor forsake you," and "Lo, I am with you alway."

And thus it dawned on me that afternoon that I had reached the point in my life where I didn't question or doubt. I accepted His decisions for my life. He knew what was right for me and He was with me. What more did I need to know?

11

A Waiting, Willing Heart

Over the years I've been made aware of many things about Christians. For the most part, they assume too much. They surmise that if a person goes to church, is kind to his parents, and lives a pretty good moral life, he's a Christian.

I think there is something in the Bible about "good works" and it has nothing to do with getting to heaven. Some of the nicest people are walking around lost as they can be.

Sometimes I get the feeling Christians are afraid to ask someone about his relationship to God. If the other person *is* a Christian, he will be proud to affirm the fact and a great one-in-the-Spirit relationship can be established. But it seems we hold back and fail to go after the ones who are so obviously without God it doesn't take a Geiger counter to confirm the fact.

I speak from experience about this assumption business. I was in this city for eight years, and not one person talked to me about the God-you relationship. Not one person told me that all my sins could be forgiven—erased.

Now, I agree, I wasn't always in places where Christians were. There's not much talk about the Lord in cocktail lounges. However, every now and then I would go to church somewhere, fill out the visitor's card, and wait for a visit. On many occasions no one called on me at all. The few who did talked about me *joining* their church. Never once, in all honesty, did anyone ever come right out and ask me, "Do you know the living Lord as your Friend?"

Perhaps it was my fault. I usually started in about how active I used to be in my church in Texas, and how I had joined the church at age fifteen. What a vast difference in being on the church roll and belonging to God!

But if I had been asked to tell how I met the Lord or to give the circumstances surrounding my "conversion," I would have stuttered more than Porky Pig.

I sometimes wonder, now, in retrospect, what I might have said. Would I have lied? Would I have hedged a bit and come up with a feasible, plausible answer? Or would I have admitted honestly that I did *not* have Christ living within me?

Knowing me, I probably would have lied. But also knowing me, after that person had gone, my old conscience would have started in. Maybe the Holy Spirit would have gone to work and I would have been spared those wasted, meaningless years.

I don't know. All things happen in due time and my time was October 10, 1968. But no one led me to Christ. He called me to Himself. I know one thing. When I see a person now, I see a soul, too, and I cannot help "but speak the things which [I] have seen and heard" (Acts 4:20).

Because God goes with me everywhere, I've had the opportunity to share Him and to feel His presence in every assignment. I take my job as state women's editor very seriously. It enables me to travel throughout the state to the large cities and to the tiny towns. I've interviewed every type person from governors' wives to the woman who owns Slap-Out Wash-Out Washeteria in Slapout, Alabama. To the people *I* see *I* am the newspaper. In the brief span of time I am with them I represent my paper; therefore, I try to leave a good impression.

Our newspaper has a slogan now, "Available When You Are." I like it. Someone might miss a radio or TV newscast but the paper is there for them to get the news when *they* have the time to read it.

I'm not too keen on some religious slogans that are around nowadays: "If your God is dead, try mine, He's alive," or, "I'm a Jesus Freak." And maybe I'm contradicting myself when I say I *do* see an obvious connection to our newspaper's slogan and the Lord—"Available When You Are." He is and He said it: "Lo, I am with you alway."

So, on my one day each week to travel within the state I remember this. I represent my paper, but I also represent God. And it's amazing how many times He comes up in my interviews. I don't start the conversation in this direction— the other fellow does. Of course, I don't change the subject!

I was interviewing a woman in South Alabama some months back and was almost finished when she said, "I'm sorry. My mind hasn't been with you today, I'm afraid. My grandson is having heart surgery tomorrow and I can't stop thinking about him."

I expressed my concern and told her I would pray for her grandson that night. She looked very surprised and asked, "Do you have time to pray with me now? I think it would help."

I put down my pad, held her hand and had a short prayer with her. After the "Amen" she looked up at me and said softly, "I can't believe a newspaper reporter would have prayed with me. But I thank you."

Driving home *I* thanked God. I thanked Him that I had been there when someone needed encouragement. I thanked Him again for my new life that every single day gives me the impetus to reach out to others. And I thanked Him for my job that brings me into contact with hundreds of people I would never have the opportunity to meet otherwise.

About a month later I received a short note in the mail from this woman. Her grandson was doing well and the doctors had assured them he could now lead a normal life.

I loved her P.S. The wordage gave me goose bumps. "Thank you for praying with me and just being *available*."

Shortly after I became a Christian I decided I wanted to go into full-time Christian service. To me this meant the mission field or full-time work as a youth director or another church-related field.

I honestly believed I could not serve God unless I was totally committed to Him. What I didn't know was that I was already totally committed to Him and that I didn't have to have a seminary degree or become a missionary.

The United States of America is in dire need of full-timers to carry out God's love and promises in schools, office buildings, factories, club meetings, and homes. If I've had any success whatsoever as one of God's ambassadors, it's because, I firmly believe, I've stayed in a secular position and maintained my enthusiasm about Him.

People expect a minister to talk about God. They expect the same of any church staff member. But when a newspaper woman gets up before a group and begins to tell of the excitement of living the God-motivated life, this seems to have a surprising impact.

God made me. I am now His child. But I have my own identity and personality and it seems to fit God's plan for me to use my talents and time outside the boundaries of any religious organization.

Every talent I have, God can and does use. I stand amazed at what He thinks up! I don't suppose I'll ever get used to the fact that He *does* use me, regardless of how inadequate I feel.

And in these last few months He's taught me much about freedom. I belong to Christ, but I am free — free in Him. And that's a large space to move around in.

It's only when we come to the end of ourselves that we come to the beginning with God. And beginning means new life. My new life is expanding and growing and encompassing more and more. I'm full time, totally committed to serving forever the God who sent His only Son to set me free and give me life — and room in which to live.

As C. T. Studd, the missionary, said, "God just wants a willing heart. Any old turnip will do for a head."

Under this standard many people would qualify if they could only catch on that God wants them — just as they are. He'll furnish the heart. Don't worry about the head!

One person who uses her heart and shows others the beauty of Christ is Freita Fuller.

I was assigned to cover the Miss Alabama Pageant — a week of writing stories and taking pictures from the first girl's arrival in our city to the televised pageant on Saturday evening.

As I looked at the thirty-four pretty contestants the first day, I thought to myself, "I really don't see how God is going to use me this week. Not at a beauty pageant." How we limit Him!

Toward the middle of the week and some fifty photographs later, I had gotten to know a few of the girls. I never had much time with them as their schedules were so tight. I just had them long enough to get a picture of each and a little something about them.

One girl, however, stood out. I had been watching Freita Fuller, a beautiful, tall, brown-haired girl from Opelika, for several days. As did all the girls, she smiled when it was picture-taking time. But I noticed Freita was smiling almost all the time. During pageant week they are a unit. You never see one girl alone. They're always with others, until the crowning on Saturday that sets one girl apart as Miss Alabama.

On Thursday afternoon I was leaving the rehearsal hall when I spotted Freita sitting with the other girls listening to State Pageant Director Janice Walker. This time she wasn't smiling and all the way back to the paper I wondered why.

I had made a trip to the Middle East earlier in the year and had bought a beautifully carved olive-wood Bible in Jerusalem. I had given away many of the things I bought on my trip, but I was determined to hang on to this Bible.

That night at home I sat in my study and tried to do some writing. For me, writing is no laborious task, but that night I strained over every sentence and made more *x*s on the paper than usual. Finally, I gave up trying to type and went to the bookshelves for something to read. There on top was my Jerusalem Bible. It was as though Freita's name was written across it and I knew it no longer belonged to me.

The next afternoon I took my note pad, camera, and Bible to my pageant assignment. As the girls were leaving for dinner, I stopped Freita long enough to hand her the Bible and say, "I don't understand why, but I feel I must give this to you."

In the evening when the girls assembled for more rehearsals, Freita's mother walked up to me and said, "You'll never know what that Bible did for Freita. She is a Christian but was beginning to lose some of her faith.

"She's dreamed of being Miss Alabama since she was old enough to know what it meant. She's tired physically and rather low. Your gift has given her a new strength and I've never seen her calmer. Thank you."

Mrs. Fuller went on to tell me Freita had polio when she was three years old. "If you'll look closely you'll see that her right leg is smaller than her left and it is two inches shorter," she said. "But she's worked hard to walk and stand so no one can notice." I had to admit I hadn't been aware. Somehow her smile raises your vision to her face and the sparkling brown eyes.

The pageant was to begin at 8 P.M. I arrived at 6:30 to get pictures of the girls putting on their makeup and getting ready for the show. Freita seemed the calmest. Once in her formal, she sat and waited for time to go on stage. One girl had the butterfly fever so bad she began to cry and Freita was the first one to her.

I said, "Let's go out in the hall. We only have a minute, but let's make use of it." Freita knew what I was thinking and she took over. The three of us held hands and Freita prayed, "God, bring peace to my friend who stands beside me. Next, thank You for the Bible that has changed my life. It was Your way of letting me know You want to use me. If being Miss Alabama is the way, that's fine. I'll speak out for You every chance I have. If I don't win, that's fine, too. I'll still give You all I have. Amen."

I left hurriedly to get a seat in the front row. I was so busy taking pictures of the pageant and making notes I didn't pay too much attention to Freita. That is, until the master of ceremonies announced the winner: "Miss Alabama is—Freita Fuller!"

I headed straight to her mother who was trying to get to her daughter, now holding a bouquet of roses and wearing the shiny crown of Miss Alabama.

"Hold on to me," I told Mrs. Fuller. "We'll get through." I held my camera over my head and we edged our way to Freita. As I stood waiting my turn to interview her I wasn't at all surprised at the things I heard her telling reporters from across the state.

"God won tonight," she said. "This is His victory. I re-dedicated my life this week and He's going to use this title of Miss Alabama."

Some reporters looked at her like she was a nut. Unlike most beauty winners Freita wasn't crying—and hadn't shed a tear. That was the headline on my own story about the new Miss Alabama: "NO TEARS FOR FREITA."

She's kept the promise she made to God in the hall before the pageant. In the Miss America Pageant in Atlantic City the judges asked her about her connection with Campus Crusade for Christ and she let go up there about how real God is to her and about her new commitment to Him.

She didn't win Miss America. She didn't place in the top ten, either. But she won anyway. She came back to Alabama and traveled thousands of miles in her capacity as Miss Alabama. She never missed an opportunity to share God and especially to reach out to teen-agers who looked at her simply as a beautiful girl. She let them know where it all came from.

From polio to pageant. It was quite a journey and Freita Fuller won both races.

There's another Miss Alabama now but there is a special section of my heart reserved just for Freita, and I will continually thank my God for every remembrance of her.

12

Unlock the Church Doors

I am in constant touch with new Christians. New, excited followers who want to "tell the world!" They seem, so many of them, to act, however, as though they alone have the secret and that they have a knowledge unknown to the rest of us.

Please do not misunderstand me. I wouldn't for the world squelch the enthusiasm of a born-again child of God. (So many of them remind me of me when I was a "year old.") I do my best to encourage them.

But I pray for them, especially, to go slowly, and learn of God with patience and not run out blindly and unprepared and "save the world."

I also know many new Christians who have real changed lives. But they suddenly become very pious and begin to see only the bad in others. And they lash out at their friends, pointing out their faults, using Scripture verses, oft times completely out of context, and people are turned off.

I would certainly be. Most people, although they may not admit them, know their faults. And they don't appreciate having a holier-than-thou new convert point them out. Too many "babes" walk before they have mastered the art of crawling.

We are not made to control Christianity; it is meant to control us. Therefore, we need to share with our friends what has happened in our life and then love them. Jesus will do the rest. We see this *if* we are maturing.

I know of one new Christian who sits home every evening reading her Bible and making lists of people to talk to. But something is missing. She looks like the most unhappy person in the world. She seems to be hung up on how bad everybody else is and gives the impression, at least to me, that God never smiles. She lives in a perpetual strain.

I think He smiles a lot. I know He has a sense of humor. Each morning when I look in the mirror I reaffirm the fact!

He didn't take away my laughter. In fact, I laugh more now. I have more to laugh about.

My new, straining Christian friend has a lot to learn. She must learn that God has to control our thoughts, our imaginations, our personalities, our actions, and our words.

Too many new ones have the wrong conception of Christianity. It is not a narrow box that we are to fit ourselves into. On the contrary, when one becomes a Christian, his world widens. My close friend, Eugenia Price, calls it, the *Wider Place.* Inviting Christ in is like setting slaves free. John 8:36 says it: "If the Son therefore shall make you free, ye shall be free indeed."

That "indeed" makes all the difference. That's emphatic and that means freedom to dislike the faults we see in others, but *love* them anyway.

I really connect with that verse that says: "God is love" (1 John 4:16). To me, that tells it all!

If God is love that doesn't give anyone the right to condemn or judge others. He told His disciples to love. *He* did, and they saw it in action every day they were with Him.

I can understand the new believer and why he zeroes in on the bad points of others. He's just been forgiven his own sins and he wants them to experience the same forgiveness. But you'll find you will get a lot more response out of non-Christians just by loving them instead of condemning them.

And smile! This will get to them quicker than anything else. I walked into an office recently, smiling broadly, and two people I know asked, "What's wrong?" I just answered back, "I'm constantly amazed that God loves me. That's all."

Christianity is a happy thing. It's really the life abundant which God promised.

Want a friend to question the difference in your life? Then smile and show him that God truly is love because He is loving through you!

The other day I asked a six-week-old Christian, a big, husky man—the type you associate with boxing gloves, football, and weight lifting—what it was about Christianity and Christ Himself that brought him to his acceptance of the Lord and to become a totally changed and enthusiastic new follower.

His answer was, "It was the challenge."

I asked him to further explain and he was more than happy to. "You see, I'd always excelled in football. It was a challenge at first, but I lost my enthusiasm after I discovered some of the tricks of the game. Even after we'd win a game, I'd feel empty somewhere inside."

He went on, "In business, my challenge was to make money and to succeed. Well, I've made money and I guess you'd say I was a success—business-wise, anyway. But, once I'd attained it, the challenge was gone and the empty feeling was still there.

"Then somebody approached me about Christ, and being a

Christian, and when I began to look into this Christian living thing, man," he said, "I saw the biggest challenge I'd ever seen! To try and live as Christ said to, to abide honestly by all His teachings—I just had to accept it. And when I did, the empty feeling went away."

This man had come to Christ because he at long last had found a challenge he knew he couldn't possibly conquer and lay aside, but a challenge that would inspire and spur him on to greater and more meaningful challenges. The God-shaped void had been filled.

Man, basically, responds to challenges. The song, "Anything You Can Do, I Can Do Better," is a part of everyone. As a child, how many times did you ever dare someone to do something difficult? How many times did you take up a challenge, even though it wasn't too bright, and do some deed to prove yourself brave or not chicken?

I remember one day old Ralph challenged me to climb to the top of our chinaberry tree. I was scared to death of heights, but I couldn't let him think I was a sissy (although my mother kept telling me girls were *supposed* to be sissies).

So, up the tree I went, never looking back until I'd reached the top limb. I looked down (second mistake—first mistake was climbing that tree in the first place) and saw my friend walking away. There I was, practically roof level with our house, butterflies coming out both my ears and "my old buddy" could have cared less.

That's not the way it is with Christ. He gives us a challenge, no matter how tough, and He's right there beside us all the way.

Jesus challenged Peter. Peter looked over the side of the boat and saw Jesus actually walking on the water.

"Now, if He can, so can I," thought Peter, so he yelled, "Wait for me" and stepped out. What happened was, he got about halfway to Jesus, took his eyes off Him, and began to sink. From the physical size of this big fisherman, I rather imagine you could have heard him across the lake, blubbering for Jesus to save him (*see* Matthew 14:28-30).

First, Peter probably *could* have walked all the way to Jesus, but he removed his vision from Him, began to think of himself, and like me, I rather imagine he might have yelled, "Look at me!" He got all involved in the fact he really *was* walking on water, lost his faith, and began to sink.

That happens to Christians every day. We start out on a task and we find we're doing a pretty fair job. So fine a job that we forget to trust completely in Christ and begin to trust our puny selves. What happens is that we fail. And so many times we say, "The Lord let me down." Not so. He's right there where He always is. He just wants us to put *all* our faith in Him.

Take a challenge from God, add prayer and a whole lot of faith, and you'll end up with something worthwhile.

I believe two words sum up the challenging nature of Jesus Christ: "Follow me." It is an invitation from the Lord, and it's up to us to respond.

About once a month I speak to the Wednesday night services at an unwed mother's home. Usual attendance at these chapel services is around fifty or sixty girls.

This is one of the highlights of my month. This is a place where Christ's love can really be told. Here sit these girls, many of them feeling pretty low about their present circumstances and wondering what life has in store for them—if anything. It's the most thrilling thing to know you can tell them what *can* be ahead for them if they give their lives to Christ.

One night after the talk, some fifteen girls came forward and kneeled at the small altar at the front of the chapel. They had been told that Jesus had said, ". . . go, and sin no more" (John 8:11). "Thy sins be forgiven thee" (Matthew 9:2). They had believed Him.

There *was* hope and they knew it. They had a new chance and they knew that, too. When Christ enters a heart, He comes in bringing a tomorrow and the past is wiped away. When Christ enters a heart He brings relief.

After refreshments, one attractive girl said she wanted to talk to me. We went into the director's office and she told me that she had given her heart to Christ that night. It was a beautiful, radiant face that looked up at me.

"It's just great," she said, "and I do feel so much better. I want to make up for so many things and I want to serve God. But I have a problem at home. When I found out I was pregnant, I went to my pastor and asked for advice. He really made me feel awful and sinful, and he told me he thought I ought to change churches because of the kind of girl I am. He was afraid I would be a bad influence on the other kids. Now, I don't know what to do. I come from a small town and that's the only church of my denomination there. I want to be of use to the Lord. If He can forgive *me,* I'll always work for Him."

She also told me many of the adults in the church had talked about her, too.

Finally, I said, "Why don't you go back to the pastor, tell him about your newfound life with Christ, let the people know, and just start working for Christ in your community? People will see the change in you. If some persist in talking, just let them. God can handle it."

"Oh, I don't know," she smiled. "I guess I don't mind the talk. And suddenly I just feel sorry for that minister! He knows so little about life, really. You see, his son is the father of my baby."

W-O-W!

I still sometimes pray for that nameless minister. I can almost see him standing up there behind his pulpit preaching hellfire and damnation to his respectable congregation. And then I wonder if he has a daughter at home.

I'm concerned about some of God's churches. Many members of congregations talk a good game about "following Jesus," "tithing," "100 percent Sunday-school attendance," "good healthy budgets," or "our new paved parking lot." But somewhere in there, discrepancies abound and many would-be members are turned off and turned out.

I make my comments from firsthand experience. A friend, Ann, was director of a college-age Sunday-school department that met in an old dingy-looking building adjacent to the church. When she first took over, approximately fifteen students came on Sunday mornings.

Having taught school and having worked with young people for ten years, she decided to try some innovative things to get the kids there. She went first and visited every dormitory on the two large university campuses in town and invited the students who didn't have a church to come to hers.

They began to come. She served coffee, hot chocolate, and doughnuts before Sunday school and the kids loved this twenty-minute "breakfast time."

Interest began to build and she grabbed hold of it and held a meeting in her home one week. At this meeting the group discussed how they could improve the old building in which they met. All came up with the idea that if they painted it, got some carpeting put down, and made it more attractive, the students would be proud to bring their friends there. Bible studies were planned, social events were set up, and rehearsals began on an original musical my friend had written. Enthusiasm was high and everybody began work on the "new building."

Paint was secured and Ann went to carpet dealers all over the city to either buy or rummage around in warehouses for carpet scraps. But, on the second visit to a carpet store, the manager became interested in Ann's story of sprucing up a place where kids could come for fellowship and Bible study.

"What kind of car are you driving?" he asked.

"A four-door sedan. Why?" she answered.

"Well, back it up to the loading dock and we'll start filling it up. If you know of anybody else with a car, better call him because I'm going to give you all the carpet squares and scraps you can carry."

His name was Mr. Lawrence and I'll never forget his generosity.

Ann called a college student she knew was home and he came to the store and began loading his car, too, with carpeting. My friend drove across town with multicolored carpeting stacked to the roof of the car in the back and front seat with just enough room left to steer the automobile with one hand. The trunk was filled to overflowing, too.

Once unloaded, the carpeting was put down, each piece nailed to the old wooden floor — a tedious job that took three days and nights with Ann staying until 4 A.M. two mornings.

The walls were bright yellow, trimmed in navy blue and with the bright carpeting, the old building was beautiful! Rusty metal folding chairs were removed and empty wooden telephone cable spools were used for tables and the kids sat on the now-carpeted floor.

Things were going fine until one evening just before a youth revival. Ann and some of the students were putting the finishing touches on the foyer in preparation for an after-revival party to be held in the new place.

Ann was on her knees nailing down the final carpet squares when she heard men's voices behind her. She turned around to see seven or eight men standing there surveying the premises.

Thinking they had come to view the redecorating job, she innocently asked, "Well, how do you like it?"

The spokesman for the group stepped forward and said, "This place looks like a nightclub. If you're going to turn this into a coffeehouse there's no telling what type people will come in here."

Voices from behind him mumbled agreement to his speech.

These were deacons of the church and sheer anger was obvious on every face. One man began to literally shake all over and his face got so red he had to go outside for air.

Soon they all left and Ann stood there holding a hammer in her limp right hand. After all the weeks of planning and actual labor, this attack was like a strong right to the midsection!

The upshot of the whole thing was that the deacons shortly asked the pastor to leave because he had encouraged my friend to do anything to get kids coming. They called him everything from communist to hippie lover.

He left and within months so did Ann, the associate pastor, and the minister of music. A quartet of dedicated, God-loving people had been asked to leave because the chances of "somebody different" coming into their church was more than they could cope with.

The building with the clean, bright walls and carpeting is empty. It could be filled to overflowing every night with people who want to learn more of God's love.

I feel quite sure boys with long hair and blue jeans *would* have begun to come to that church. They would also have sat in the pews near those deacons and these men didn't want "that kind."

From my own personal conception of Jesus Christ, He would have probably met them at the front door. Many church members lose sight of Christ's vision and purpose. *He came to find lost sheep,* not to make churches showplaces for "saints." And it startles me when I consider the number of youths who were planning to visit that church but never had the opportunity. They simply would not have been welcome. They didn't conform to these church members' conception of what a person should look like.

That red man is alive and working in our churches today. It's a good field for him because the house of God is the place where people can come to know Christ. At least they are subjected to His Word and even though sometimes poorly presented, God still gets through. The devil's presence in that church is the only way I can explain to myself the actions of some of the people in the congregation. I saw love just leave people and real honest-to-goodness hate take over.

Many of those kids not only looked like hippies, they were. But they had openly admitted they were searching for something beyond the drug scene. They were beginning to get excited about Jesus Christ!

In the beginning they weren't interested in how they looked. That would come later. They wanted a personal experience with God and many had expressed it just that way.

Christ loved. Oh, how He loved! And it is nothing less than tragic when church leaders remain so rigid that they close their minds and their hearts to ones who need love most.

I saw a boy recently with shoulder-length hair who had visited this church. I spoke to him and he said, "Better not speak to me. I'm a vacuum cleaner."

I asked what he meant and he had tears in his eyes when he answered. "I walked in that church and sat down and people cleared out four and five pews on either side of me. I just wanted love, man. Just love."

He turned away and walked off down the street singing "Jesus loves me . . . ."

13

And All Creatures Therein

I was sent on an assignment once to report on a baby owl that had fallen from a tree and was now a house pet.

As I drove to the interview I laughed to myself, "On-the-spot coverage of six-week-old owl! You really get the hot news, Norman!"

Fuzzy, the baby owl, turned out to be more of a story than I had thought. To be perfectly honest, I've never liked birds. Their little feet moving on my arm made my skin crawl. But Fuzzy was different. He flew to my shoulder, snuggled close to my neck, and just sat there throughout the interview with Fuzzy's human family.

The more those people talked of the things this little creature could do, the more I caught myself snuggling back. I loved a bird!

Fuzzy ate hamburger meat, sat on the back of the den sofa and watched television, rode on the front of the family's boat, and loved to go for automobile rides.

I had the story. I needed the photograph. He was so cute I

wanted to capture him on film. I was afraid a picture of Fuzzy in the newspaper would appear only as a little furry ball.

I asked if there was an owl cookie jar in the house. There was. I sat Fuzzy next to his look-alike and snapped one picture. The flash did the trick. Fuzzy stood to his full height of four inches and stared at the light. I continued to snap away.

Back at the newspaper I typed the story while my film was being processed. I had just finished and was rereading when Fuzzy's portrait came down. I must call it a portrait because that's exactly what it was!

I was looking at the photo when one of the senior editors came by. He looked at Fuzzy standing proudly next to his ceramic relative and said, "Page one."

My mundane assignment had turned into my first page-one story. On the following day I proudly viewed Fuzzy and the accompanying story, center stage of our newspaper.

Not long after, I learned the photo had been nominated for an award and although Fuzzy didn't win first place, the whole thing was a thrill for me.

All this took place over a year ago and just last week I received a letter from the little girl who owned Fuzzy. It was a short note, but it said enough: "I thought you might like to know," she wrote, "that Fuzzy died yesterday. We didn't know he was sick. He just died. Thank you for writing about my pet. I loved him and I miss him."

I put down the note, went to the lounge, and said a special prayer for that child. I know Fuzzy was an owl but to her he was something to love. And that owl loved back.

I returned to my desk and looked out at the city room, noisy and lively as ever. There had been a robbery in town and the place was jumping. Reporters and photographers were being sent out and the police radio was blaring. This was a big deal and I knew it would fill page one the following day.

My little owl seemed so insignificant as I looked at the note written in a child's handwriting laying on my desk. Somehow I felt cut off from all the sounds of the moment.

I remembered a story I had written about a dog; one about a turtle that did tricks, and an article I had written on a kitten that rolled over and played dead. These weren't the "biggies," but Fuzzy had brought them all back to memory. They seemed to march across my typewriter paper like the animal crackers I'd line up against my window as a child. I became aware that God loves all His creations — big and little — and I didn't feel a bit silly for sitting there thinking about my friends in the smaller world.

Then I thought, "God, I'm so glad You live inside me. Despite all the action going on in the newspaper, You've given me the ability to love and feel for everything including the Fuzzys of the world. Don't let me ever stop caring for the big things in life, but especially the small. Especially the small."

Assignments, like with Fuzzy, sometimes turn into a special surprise. On the other hand, some stories come from just being in the right place at the right time. How was I to know that my membership in the Birmingham AERO Club would lead to one of my most unforgettable experiences in reporting?

An annual event for us was the AERO Club Air Show. That year we had a record crowd and the caliber of the show was superb. I was asked to make movies of the show so I found myself a front-row seat on a flatbed truck near the runway. The star attraction of the day was Chuck Hale, an accomplished, popular aerobatic. Earlier in the day, I had watched Chuck warm up and he and the wild blue yonder had a personal relationship that made them one. He did fantastic spins, triple loops, rolls, nose dives, and through my zoom lens he looked like a giant blue mosquito that had gone swimming in a glass of straight gin. Chuck Hale didn't ride in an airplane. He strapped the seat belt on and the plane just went along for the fun.

He was the last act on the program and, once in the sky, there was an eerie quiet that fell over the crowd. They didn't applaud and cheer as they had the other flyers. When Chuck took his plane straight up, stalled, then began spinning earthward, they sat as one person, afraid any noise would spoil the almost reverent atmosphere that prevailed.

I felt the same way. Several times I caught myself watching him through my lens and suddenly realized I wasn't taking pictures. I was spellbound by his agility and control of that plane.

Chuck zoomed down near a row of trees on the other side of the runway, did a snap roll, and disappeared behind the trees. He had zipped behind those trees all afternoon and we waited for the blue plane to soar up again. What came up over those trees was not a blue plane.

First, it was a muffled thud, then bellows of black smoke, and then red flames.

All I knew to do was keep that camera going. For a split second after the crash everyone seemed suspended. No one moved. Then a fire truck started out toward the smoke, followed by several doctors who are members of the AERO Club, and several medics from the National Guard.

Someone, I don't know who, got to the public address system and made an announcement that stilled the crowd that by now was reacting to what had happened before their eyes. Many were crying. Some just stood and stared. The announcer said, "Due to the fatal crash of Chuck Hale the air show is over. Everyone please leave in as orderly a way as possible."

I shut off the camera and looked at the guy holding the microphone. That word *fatal* had penetrated my own concentration of the scene. The doctors hadn't even had time to reach

Chuck. I realized it *looked* impossible that the man could be alive, but the announcer aired a pretty premature assumption.

People all around me began speaking in terms of "Chuck *was* a fine man"; "He'll be missed"; "How that guy loved to fly. That *was* his life." And other such talk. I don't remember any more. For everyone at the show, Chuck was dead and it surprised me how quickly people accepted it.

About ten minutes later we saw movement in the trees and through my zoom lens I saw men carrying a stretcher and the body on the stretcher was waving. Chuck Hale was alive!

An army helicopter was standing by to fly Chuck to University Hospital in Birmingham and soon it lifted off the ground and became a tiny speck in the sky.

In all the confusion I had given no thought to the paper, but realized I must get back to the airport office and call in. I called the city room and told them there had been a crash and Chuck Hale was injured, probably seriously, but was alive. "Send a reporter out here to cover this," I said. A very solemn voice answered back with, "What do you think *you* are? Handle it and get down here as soon as you've got something."

Although the party on the other end of the line had already hung up, I stood there holding the phone saying, "But, but . . . ." I'd been told to "handle it" and that meant get the story.

I didn't even have a note pad with me. I looked in my purse, found an old airline ticket and used that to record my information. I got a few remarks from the builder and designer of Chuck's plane, talked to some of the first ones to reach Chuck, and found out the real story.

When they reached him they found his plane had crashed in the trees (breaking his fall) and then droppped into a swamp. Chuck was lying half in, half out of the cockpit and when the first person got to him he grinned and said, "You know, sometimes these things aren't very safe." An initial examination disclosed a fractured leg, severe burns on his face, arms, and legs, and possible back damage.

In actuality, Chuck had saved his own life. He never lost consciousness. When he hit he realized he was on fire, unbuckled the seat belt, crawled out of the cockpit, and began splashing swamp water on himself to put out the fire. Then he just waited for somebody to reach him.

I knew I had to get to the hospital. Traffic was lined up for miles. A friend came up to me and said, "I've got a sports car. I believe we can make better time. Let's go."

At the hospital I saw Chuck's family in the waiting room. The doctor had just told Mrs. Hale her husband would live but further X rays were needed to give the full extent of injuries. She was holding up her husband's watch and said to me happily, "Look, it's still running and the crystal isn't even broken."

Spirits were high and I joined in their celebration of the miracle of the day. I got a few facts from Mrs. Hale and went to the paper to write my story. I sat looking at a blank sheet of paper in my typewriter and didn't know where to begin.

The deadline for the story pushed me into getting it done. The photographs came down and I turned in my account of the crash of Chuck Hale.

I went back to my desk and thought since I was at the paper I would work on my column for the next day. I typed a few inches but my mind began to wander back to the events of the afternoon.

The astonishing fact Chuck had come out of that crash alive was obvious. I remembered then that I hadn't taken time to thank God. So I did. Then I saw a real comparison to what had happened to Chuck and an event in Jesus' life.

When Jesus was put on the cross His enemies knew they

had at last put an end to this "troublemaker." Nobody had ever walked away from a cross and they had Him exactly where they wanted Him. He Himself spoke the words, "It is finished" (John 19:30), and He died. His disciples wept and His foes celebrated. Jesus of Nazareth was a fatality!

I'm sure the word was shouted and spread rapidly that "He is dead!" Despite the fact He had said He would return, He was dead and it was accepted.

The mourning *and* the jubilance was soon to come to an end. The stone was rolled away and a new shout was heard. This time it came from His followers and they let go with, "He is alive! He is alive!"

Jesus' enemies surely must have announced, as did the man that Sunday: "Due to the death of Jesus of Nazareth, the show is over. Everyone please leave in as orderly a way as possible."

A premature assumption! Little did they know the "show" was just beginning and the Star Attraction was still alive where He would forever remain.

I turned back to my typewriter and zipped through three columns with the beautiful fact in my heart that "He *is* alive!"

14

Who Can I Turn To?

In previous chapters I've talked about spiritual boldness and looking for the lost sheep—in a word, witnessing.

But I believe there is a *way* to witness. I pray some day I will find that perfect way to lay out God's wonderful blueprints before someone in an effective manner.

I have seen so many truly sincere Christians, armed with tracts, attacking, and I meant to use that exact word—*attacking* people with the Gospel of Christ. I could see it hit them wrong. It hit *me* wrong and *I* knew what the Christian was talking about. The text of the conversation is not always what turns people off, but the manner in which it is presented.

I know when a salesman appears at my door and comes on strong, giving his pitch without coming up for air, I simply become disinterested. I wouldn't have time to ask a question if I could find a place to interject one. *And,* I wouldn't buy his product. You see, I would be so involved with the person and his approach that I wouldn't buy what he had to sell even though it might be something I really needed.

As I see it, the approach is what turns off so many would-be Christians. I've talked about enthusiasm, but when you are witnessing to someone in need of Christ, don't use the kind of enthusiasm a wrestler uses on his opponents. Strangleholds will never show anyone the love and beauty of Jesus Christ.

For over a year, I'd been consistently praying for a friend, trying to show God's love and all the peace this love gives. He had only memories of another me. It was a hard row, but he began to listen as I talked of the Man who walked the earth and died for His "lost sheep."

Once he piped up with, "Hey, you talk like He's Somebody you really know. I mean like He's your next door neighbor or something."

I at least had him talking and I told him that I *did* know Him and "He lives a lot closer than next door. He lives in my heart."

We had similar conversations. Each time *he* brought up the subject and I could tell he was becoming interested.

Then, one evening, a layman friend stopped by. I introduced the two and this layman's first words were, "If you died tonight would you go to heaven or hell?"

I'm sorry my friend was rude, but he answered with, "I guess I'd go to hell. Especially if heaven is going to be full of people like you." Out the door he walked.

We had fewer conversations after that and never did they even hint at Christianity. I've seen my friend and other people just tune out when this is the *first* question put to them by a witnessing Christian.

I've heard non-Christians talk and they get livid about this kind of "disciple." Nobody wants to feel he is being pushed or scared into anything or shoved in a corner and told, "Open wide, buddy. You're about to become a Christian."

I wonder how many Christians earnestly pray before they

go out to talk to someone about the Lord? The Bible says, "Take no thought how or what you shall speak: for it shall be given you in that same hour what you shall speak."

Exactly right! If we have paved the way with humble prayers, admitting we don't know what to say, or *how* to say it, God will give the right words to say, *and* the manner in which to say them.

Christianity is so positive. I like to think of it as *affirmative* living. There are so many good things to tell the non-Christian. Share with him your own testimony and fulfilling life with God. Let the person know the peace and happiness you experience every day from living the affirmative life. Let him know he'll never be alone again—God will always be there. Point out that *all* his sins can be forgiven, and he can start over as a new person. And don't leave out the great part of living in heaven for eternity with the Lord.

By this point, if you have his interest, and you should— you've told him nothing but good things—*then* give him the consequences of rejecting Him. Tell him that no man can make it to heaven except through Christ and that there is salvation in no other manner. Tell him that he is condemned already "because he hasn't believed in the name of the only begotten Son of God."

I'm a good one to talk, you say? I have a lot to learn, but by studying God's Word daily I am more and more convinced that Jesus Himself never high-pressured anyone. He told them the Way, simply and very plainly, but He never grabbed anybody by the throat and insisted they swallow His teachings.

I believe a good thing for many Christians to do is simply read very carefully the New Testament and be aware of how *Jesus* acted—how He handled situations—how He dealt with those who didn't agree with Him.

His messages to the people didn't always have three points.

He didn't repeat and repeat. He didn't insist the people make decisions on the spot. He simply (oh, the beauty of His simplicity!) said things via illustrations and parables and then left for another town. He didn't belabor points. He forced no one. He loved. He *was* love and the impact of that love has endured for two thousand years. Too many good-intentioned Christians foul up things by interjecting self into their witness. We need to step aside and let God take over.

"The harvest truly is great, but the labourers are few . . ." (Luke 10:2).

The harvest truly is great, and may God's laborers be well-equipped with the spirit of truth, compassion, and a good sense of timing.

I saw a Christian today doing her thing, and it wasn't a very pretty thing.

This attractive woman came barreling into an office demanding information. She literally jerked the telephone out of one of the worker's hands. She was abrupt, curt. I thought to myself (I didn't know at the time she was a Christian) what a rude person she was.

On her way out the door, she stopped, smiled, and made some sugary comments about the fine work being done in the office and left a religious tract on the desk nearest the door. Everyone just sat and stared after her. Someone said, *"And she's been saved!"*

What an ache I had in the pit of my stomach. What a hurt I felt for Christ that one of His representatives should and *did* act in such a manner. Some of us act like spiritual idiots.

Don't you see how very important it is to be *aware* of being a Christian? More damage was done in the two or three minutes that woman spent in that office than could be done by any agnostic standing on a soapbox, speaking out *against* God.

She's a new Christian and she is excited about her new life, but just like all of us, there is so much of the old to combat. Excitement and zeal are wonderful assets, but some just need a little finer tuning in to God's wavelength, to God's way of doing things.

Christ talked about denying oneself and taking up a cross and following Him.

To *deny* oneself means to get rid of the ego, and this woman appeared to have been eaten up with the stuff. Most of her conversation contained a great many "I's." Although she was attractive physically, she left a bad impression. And her well-meaning tract hit the trash can.

If the things we do are done with *our* motivations behind them, then we cannot say we are serving God. It doesn't matter if the things concern working for a church project, leading a youth group, teaching a Sunday-school class, or even preaching. Because if self is the reason for doing something, and the purpose to show others how good you are, be informed you're not fooling God, nor serving Him. Everything we do *must* be for the glory of God and to see that He gets all the credit. If any other reason is involved, face up to the motivation and aim toward getting it God-centered.

God gives us many talents. Some can sing, play instruments, speak, get jobs done that others do not have the organizational mind to do. But these talents must be given to Him along with ourselves or they are of no value to God. The *self* goes to God first, then the talents tag along, and God will use them as *He* sees fit. He *will* use them—perhaps not in the way *you* would use them, but that is part of the greatness of being sold out to Christ—watching and experiencing God working in our lives, using us and our talents in ways we never could dream up.

Too many well-meaning Christians rush in where angels would not *dare* tread, and they give God, or other Christians, the church, and even Christianity, a bad name. We do not need this kind of publicity. Non-Christians just eat it up. That's what they are looking for—weak, useless, foolish, proud, ineffective Christians.

Many wear the name Christian, but they're not all alike. Just because you're born in a garage doesn't mean you're a car.

You can't put a Christian on a flannel board and say, "This is what a Christian looks like." We come in all shapes, sizes, colors, and brain capacities. There is no set mold you can put a man into and have him come out A CHRISTIAN. It should be so simple!

My next-door neighbor's child got a toy for Christmas called "Incredible Edible." The box has many different varieties of molds in it. You mix up this colored gook, pour it into a mold, bake it for so many minutes, open up the mold, and you have a little frog, or bug, or some strange-looking thing. What's even worse, the child eats it. He's supposed to. It's harmless gook.

Being a Spirit-filled, effective Christian is no easy task; many people would love to find a giant mold, step in, inhale some gook, bake a few minutes, and emerge a ready-made Dwight L. Moody. That *would* be easy! But that's not how the Bible says we are to be molded.

We are to put our lives into God's hands, exercising complete trust and faith, and He'll do the molding. And we won't emerge an "Incredible Edible," either. We won't really ever emerge or evolve into a finished product, for God's molding process goes on and on. We change and are reshaped, but it's not the work of a few minutes' baking.

I've given a bad impression many times, I know. I've had to go home and really pray. If we would do more praying *beforehand* and more "waiting on the Lord," there just might be more takers for Christ.

Christian, face the very important fact you no longer belong to yourself. You belong to God. You were bought with a price and it wasn't a cheap one. Stop trying to run things *your* way and let Christ take over. Think more in terms of "I've prayed about this thing. I've turned it over to God and I'm confident that the thing I have done will glorify Him."

". . . lean not unto thine own understanding" (Proverbs 3:5). You see, God's way is so much better. *And,* He would have it that way.

I was driving down the highway the other day. I heard a song on the radio that has bothered me ever since. The tune is nice. The words are horribly pessimistic.

I'm wondering how many people in the world today feel like the title of this song: "Who Can I Turn To." It's a song about a poor fellow who feels nobody needs him. He says he "must go where destiny leads him."

A follower of Christ need never go where fate, or the wind, or destiny leads him. First of all, he knows ultimately where he is going. At times, though doubts and frustrations may hang in there, he knows who holds the world.

"The Lord is my shepherd" (Psalms 23:1), and like sheep we must follow faithfully the Keeper of the flocks, always putting our trust in Him. It would indeed be frightening to know my own life was left to destiny or to chance, or to the belief that "whatever will be will be."

It has been said so many times, I know, but it is still new to me: "I don't know what tomorrow holds, but I *do* know who holds tomorrow." God holds our lives in the palms of His hands. We are His sheep and though the road toward your future is often rocky, you are eternally safe, for Jesus Christ, not destiny, is leading you.

This song also speaks of the darkness hiding us. Hidden in darkness. What a depressing mental picture. This brings to mind the contact I've had with teen-age drug users and this part of the song reminds me all too vividly of them. They exist, not *live,* through each day, awaiting the darkness when they can escape with others like themselves to man-made caves of darkness, illumined only by strange-colored lights, pulsating to an even stranger sound of what they call the NOW.

And the darkness does hide them. In fact, it swallows them up.

I went to a place where all the kids there, and they *were* kids, were "turned on." I call it "turned off." They walked, or sat, or leaned, zombielike, and stared. Someone switched on a light and two or three yelled out, "Man, douse it. It's killing my eyes."

I thought about the verse, ". . . men [love] darkness rather than light . . ." (John 3:19). But I also thought of all those children as *souls,* and another verse came to me: ". . . though I walk through the valley of the shadow . . . I will fear no evil: for thou art with me . . ." (Psalms 23:4).

How I would have loved to have gotten up on a tabletop and told them this—that God could grab them out of that pit of darkness and give them light and life, and they could be "new creatures" in the biblical sense. But they wouldn't have heard me. One young man kept insisting he was riding on a cloud and got angry because I said I couldn't see his cloud.

He kept repeating, "Maybe if you look real hard you can see it," or, "I think maybe it might not really be a cloud after all."

Maybe. The indefiniteness of that word! The frustration of wanting something, looking for things that aren't there but hoping *maybe.* Ask anyone what he really wants from life and you'll find that happiness and contentment are always named. They can't be found in *maybe.* That's what is so terrific about belonging to God. It is positive and definite. No *maybe.* ". . . for I know whom I have believed . . ." (2 Timothy 1:12).

This same song goes on to talk flippantly about forgetting sorrows and obtaining happiness and laughter in any way they can be found. Laugh and the world laughs with you. Ha! The odds are more in favor of the world laughing at you. Because if all you are after is fake, surface or forced laughter, you are a fool. From ages past the world has laughed at fools.

Sorrow cannot be thrown off with a laugh. It can be relieved *only* by Jesus Christ and complete belief in Him. "Cast all your cares upon Him, for He cares for you." That means *all* your sorrows, too.

"Who can I turn to?" you ask. There *is* no one but Christ. You see, no one else ever died on a cross and then walked away from the tomb. Only Christ. And *He* won't turn away from *you*. "I will never leave thee, nor forsake thee" (Hebrews 13:5). If anyone turns, it will be *us*. I have never thought of how the back of Jesus looked, because I have always imagined Him facing me. He stands facing you. He will not turn away.

Sometimes the most unlikely people do turn away. I interviewed an ex-minister some months past and still recall the time spent with him.

I've found that generally, fanatical ex-alcoholics, ex-smokers, or ex-anythingers can be obnoxious. I'm always thrilled when someone kicks a habit they feel has been bad for them, but sometimes people can be bores. This man is ex-God and his arguments are as flimsy as silk.

I don't remember how we got on the subject of God. I had gone to interview him about his antique car collection. I probably asked him what his profession was and that triggered our talk.

"I used to be a minister," he said rather piously, "but chucked the whole thing over a year ago. I really began to doubt the existence of God and now after much research and thought I feel man is an entity unto himself."

He sat on the fender of a shiny yellow Model T and began to really "preach" to me. "Whatever man has achieved, he's done it by himself, using his own mind. I believe Christianity makes simpletons of men. It seeks to take away our individual, personal knowledge and limits us to rules set down by God. I believe strongly that man is the maker of his own destiny."

I finished my interview, told him it was "interesting" to have met him and left. All my talking seemed to have no impression on him; however, it caused me to do a lot of thinking on the drive home!

I had to agree with my ex-minister friend in that man *has* come far. He *is* an intelligent being. But God created man and gave him the brains to be intelligent. In the world we live in, we are witnessing technological achievements at which our grandfathers would have scoffed.   .

I thought about man's brain and what he has accomplished on this earth, to — ironically — get away from the earth. Man has been to the moon. Now he talks of going beyond to Mars. So he makes it to Mars. The inquisitive mind of man will not stop there. He will make bigger and tougher rockets that will shoot him into vast regions of our solar system yet unknown.

"In the beginning God created the heaven and the earth" (Genesis 1:1). All that space out there belongs to God. It's His own creation and man is just now beginning to scratch the surface. Our voyages to the moon have been fantastic and I admire and respect the brave men who rode those rockets and walked on the moon's surface.

I had the opportunity to speak personally with two of the astronauts who have set foot on the moon, and both talked of how much *more* aware of God they are now. They had been up there in His heavens, seen the beauty He created, and I sensed they felt a little like intruders.

Astronaut James Irwin said, "After my journey to the moon,

I am more convinced and excited than ever — God made it all. I felt His presence everywhere."

Man is an achiever. I still don't understand how a television set works. To be perfectly honest, I don't even understand the fundamentals of a radio. Without the *on-off* switch, I'd be in trouble.

I believe in giving credit where it is due and man *is* intelligent. But in the *beginning* was God! In the *now* is God! In the *forever* will be God!

Time passed quickly on the drive back home and just before I turned into my driveway I prayed that the man I had interviewed would discover God. He *is* knowable and He *is* real. Encounters with people like this man only strengthen my faith. I'm so glad I am not the maker of my own destiny.

"He was before all else began and it is his power that holds everything together" (Colossians 1:17 LB).

That's heavy.

15

He Lives

He lives, He lives, Christ Jesus lives today!
He walks with me and talks with me
   along life's narrow way.
He lives, He lives, salvation to impart!
You ask me how I know He lives?
He lives within my heart.
                              — A. H. Ackley

Here I am at the last chapter. Now, I really want to be truth-
ful with you. While writing this book I've kept a part of my
mind (see how versatile?) thinking about the superspectacular
ending I was going to lay on you. Like when you close the back
cover you dash starry-eyed to the telephone and order a full-
page color ad to be run in your local newspaper admonishing
everyone to read this book.

Or, renaming all your children after Old Testament prophets
or mountains in the Holy Land. (So what's wrong with a name
like Ararat Smith?)

Or maybe surprising your husband by selling the house,

car, furniture—everything, and coyly saying, "Honey, I've just read this *marvelous* book and I've sold all we have, given the money to the poor (my parents), and volunteered us to go to China as missionaries. We leave tomorrow."

All this is done, of course, what else, with a host of angels singing the Hallelujah Chorus in the background.

No, that won't work. First of all, it's far too optimistic on my part (the full-page color ad would help, though), and it might cause dissension in your family.

I think I'll go wash my hair and maybe with my head immersed under water something will come to me.

Okay, I'm back. I got a couple of thoughts but the only major thing that happened was I forgot and took the manuscript in the shower with me. If your book is a bit damp, I'm sorry. Open it and put it face down on the water heater. I dry out my wet newspapers this way.

No, I think I'll just be honest with you and tell you exactly what I'm thinking now that fourteen chapters are behind me and a great part of my life. Permit me to share what I'm thinking as I wind up this very personal assignment with *you*.

Everything is new now. But I must look back on those old memories and be thankful for them, too. I wouldn't want to relive a single minute of them, but I am awfully glad God let me go my own way. You can see things a lot clearer when you come out of a dense fog into sunshine.

God bless the beautiful Christians who have always been active in church and have faithfully served God all their lives—never sidetracking to see how the world lives.

As for me, I'm glad the Lord let me have all the experiences I've had. They have taught me to be a whole lot more tolerant and understanding, not so easily shocked, and to put myself in the other guy's place because I've been there, too.

I have had college kids, and adults as well, open up to me, simply because, I believe, they knew that once I was where they were at the time. We are all interested in a product that is guaranteed—that works, that is good for a lifetime. They can see through my new attitude that God can and still does work miracles.

I don't recall how many times I have listened to someone pouring out his heart, and there I sit saying, "I know, I know." And I *do* know. But then I can give them the good news that Christ came to earth for sinners like *us,* and they can have new life and joy right in that moment.

I am not proud of any of the things I have done, but I find they come in very handy sometimes when I run across someone who feels nobody understands or believes no one can be so "bad."

I have new eyes, and most of all, a new heart. Not like these modern heart transplants, but a brand *new* heart. And the one Christ gave me will not go through this rejection business. Furthermore, this heart will never die for it is the heart of God.

Thousands of writers have attempted to describe Jesus, tell of His miracles, and explain His teachings. These things are not in this book. I wanted to tell, as simply and honestly as I could, how *I* found Christ, what has transpired in my life since that discovery, and hopefully, interest you to find Him, too.

I am no theologian, but I do know Jesus Christ. He is alive in me. And because He is, "I can do all things" (Philippians 4:13), for He will give me the strength.

Now, in looking back, I still can see the little girl with the jump rope, and the tipsy adult dropping dimes in pay telephones. But I no longer have to do things to prove myself. That confrontation back in 1968 brought a security to me I never had before. I don't yell, "Look at me! Look at me!" anymore either.

Look at Him! He's the Answer.

I know.